MICHELANGELO

for KIDS

His Life and Ideas

with **21** Activities

Simonetta Carr

CHICAGO REVIEW PRESS

Published by Chicago Review Press Incorporated
814 North Franklin Street
Chicago, Illinois 60610
ISBN 978-1-61373-193-2

Library of Congress Cataloging-in-Publication Data
Names: Carr, Simonetta, author.
Title: Michelangelo for kids : his life and ideas, with 21 activities /Simonetta Carr.
Description: Chicago, Illinois : Chicago Review Press, 2016. | Includes bibliographical references and index.
Identifiers: LCCN 2015038458 | ISBN 9781613731932 (paperback)
Subjects: LCSH: Michelangelo Buonarroti, 1475–1564—Juvenile literature. | Michelangelo Buonarroti, 1475–1564—
    Psychology—Juvenile literature. | Artists—Italy—Biography—Juvenile literature. | Renaissance—Italy—
    Juvenile literature. | BISAC: JUVENILE NONFICTION / Biography & Autobiography / Art | JUVENILE
    NONFICTION / Biography & Autobiography / Historical. | JUVENILE NONFICTION / Art / History.
Classification: LCC N6923.B9 C375 2016 Y DDC 759.5—dc23 LC record available at http://lccn.loc.gov/2015038458

Cover and interior design: Monica Baziuk
Cover images: Front cover (counterclockwise from top): Michelangelo, *The Creation of Adam*, Erich Lessing / Art Resource,
NY; Michelangelo, *David*, Galleria dell'Accademia, Dan Dicello, with the authorization of the Italian Ministry of
Cultural Heritage and Activities and Tourism; *The Conversion of Saint Paul*, Scala / Art Resource, NY; Giuliano Bugiardini,
Portrait of Michelangelo with Turban, Scala / Art Resource, NY; St. Peter's dome courtesy Pipopipo, Flickr. Back cover (top
to bottom): Sistine Chapel ceiling, Erich Lessing / Art Resource, NY; dome of the Medici Chapel, Jay8085, Flickr;
Michelangelo, *Pietà*, Alinari / Art Resource, NY.
Interior illustrations: Jim Spence
Interior maps: Erichsen Group

Printed in the United States of America

5   4   3   2   1

To my amazing, creative,
and supportive family

CONTENTS

✝

NOTE TO READERS

What if someone wanted to write a biography about you without ever talking to you? Maybe they have some of your e-mails, have seen you a few times, and can read what you post on social media. They might even be able talk to someone who knows you. Do you think their biography will be accurate? It might come very close to the truth, but it will always be incomplete. Writing a biography with insufficient information represents a great challenge for an author.

This is always the case, in varying degrees, when authors write about someone who is now dead—especially if this person lived many centuries ago. Authors read letters written by or to the person (direct correspondence) or about the person (indirect correspondence) and look for any other documents they can find—birth, marriage, and death certificates; wills; bank statements; and even shopping lists.

They also read about the times and locations in which their subject lived, and study biographies of other people who lived in similar historical and socioeconomic conditions. Then they try to put all the pieces of the puzzle together.

Of course, authors base much of their work on the writings of other biographers, especially those who lived at the same time or just after their subject. They look at how other biographers interpreted the same information and compare their conclusions, keeping in mind that biographies become less reliable as we go back in time, because fairness and accuracy have not always been as important as they are today.

The same challenges face those who want to study Michelangelo's life. His early life was not well documented, even though two of his biographies were written while he was still alive—something extremely unusual at that time. One of these biographies was authored by his friend and fellow artist Giorgio Vasari, and the other by his pupil Ascanio Condivi. Condivi's biography was practically dictated by Michelangelo.

Since these works were written by men who knew him well, modern biographers may initially think they are reliable sources. In reality, later research has discovered many inaccuracies in these writings. Michelangelo himself covered up, modified, or embellished some facts—for different reasons. While these biographies remain the starting point for any serious study of the artist, they need to be taken with a grain of salt. You can keep this in mind when you see them quoted in this book.

The great variety of opinions and interpretations of Michelangelo's life, art, and poetry is, however, far from discouraging. And this exciting field of discovery is enriched by the unusually large number of letters and documents by, to, and about Michelangelo. This is probably why so many have tried to discover the true Michelangelo, and why the search is still open—even to you.

TIME LINE

1475 ⊹ Michelangelo Buonarroti is born in Caprese, Italy, on March 6

1481 ⊹ Michelangelo's mother, Francesca, dies

1485 (circa) ⊹ Michelangelo attends school

1487 ⊹ He works as an apprentice to the painter Domenico Ghirlandaio

1490–92 (circa) ⊹ He works and lives in the Medici household

1494–95 ⊹ He leaves Florence and lives in Bologna with a new patron for nine months

1495 ⊹ He returns to Florence, where he carves a statue of a cupid and sells it as an antique

1496 ⊹ His deception is discovered, so he moves to Rome and wins the trust of a new patron

1498–99 ⊹ He carves his first and most famous *Pietà*, which is immediately recognized as a masterpiece

1501 ⊹ He returns to Florence, where he receives the commission to carve the *David*

1504 ⊹ He completes the *David*, gaining international acclaim

1505 ⊹ Pope Julius II summons Michelangelo to Rome to create his papal tomb; Michelangelo spends eight months in the quarries of Carrara selecting marble

1505–08 ⊹ After an argument with Julius II, Michelangelo asks for his pardon; Julius keeps him in Bologna for two years to carve a bronze statue

1508 ⊹ Michelangelo returns to Florence until Julius II asks him to paint the ceiling of the Sistine Chapel

1508–12 ⊹ Michelangelo works in the Sistine Chapel

1515–34 ✛	Michelangelo works mostly for the Medici family in Florence, designing the San Lorenzo facade, then designing and working on the Medici Chapel and the Laurentian Library
1534 ✛	Michelangelo leaves Florence for political reasons and moves permanently to Rome
1536–41 ✛	Pope Paul III hires Michelangelo to paint *The Last Judgment* in the Sistine Chapel; the painting gains both acclaim and criticism
1538 ✛	Michelangelo begins working on the Capitoline Hill
1542 ✛	At Paul III's request, Michelangelo paints two frescoes in the Pauline Chapel
1545 ✛	The tomb of Julius II is completed
1547 ✛	Michelangelo is appointed chief architect at both St. Peter's and the Farnese Palace
1547–55 ✛	He works on a statue known as *Florentine Pietà*, intended for his own tomb, but he nearly destroys it before completing it
1556 ✛	He begins to work on his final statue, known as *Rondanini Pietà*
1561 ✛	Pope Pius IV commissions Michelangelo to design Porta Pia (a city gate)
1563 ✛	Michelangelo designs the church of Santa Maria degli Angeli inside a portion of the ancient Diocletian baths
1564 ✛	Michelangelo dies on February 18 at his home in Rome, surrounded by friends; his nephew arranges for his body to be secretly taken to Florence and buried with great honors

INTRODUCTION

Michelangelo—An Artist to Discover

Sharing author Mark Twain's astonishment in discovering Michelangelo's contributions to the arts and architecture of every Italian city they visited, a fellow traveler jokingly blurted out to their guide, "Enough, enough, enough! Say no more! Lump the whole thing! Say that the Creator made Italy from designs by Michael Angelo!"

Michelangelo's contemporaries expressed similar feelings of awe. His biographer Giorgio Vasari wondered how Adam's figure on the ceiling of the Sistine Chapel could be produced "by the brush and design of a mortal man." Today, 500 years later, Michelangelo's quest and passion for perfection, depth, and originality continues to surprise even casual observers. Michelangelo was definitely the most renowned artist of the Italian Renaissance. He has been called, probably accurately, the greatest artist who has ever lived.

There is, however, much more to explore about this cultural giant: he was, among other things, an insightful poet, a skilled architect, and an innovative engineer. In everything he did, he continued to explore and master new techniques. Besides, during his long life (89 years, twice as long as most of his contemporaries) he was both a witness and an active participant in a series of momentous historical events that shook and transformed Europe.

He is one of the best documented artists in the world. Today, 500 of his letters are still available, as well as about 900 more written about him by his contemporaries. He has also left behind about 300 poems and 300 pages of miscellaneous writings. Besides his well-known works of art, there are about 600 drawings and sketches he most likely didn't want anyone to see. In fact, in his passion for perfection, he destroyed many more.

This abundance of documents and works, combined with the many questions still unanswered about his life, give us a fascinating image of a man who redefined the concept of artist and both set new standards and opened doors for others to follow. A study of Michelangelo and his works could easily occupy a lifetime, with hardly a dull moment.

This book will help you along the journey. You will follow Michelangelo from his childhood to his last years, through his many aspirations, struggles, victories, and regrets. You will learn about people, events, and places that affected his life and work, and will see how his art has continued to inspire artists and viewers all over the world.

✠ AN ✠ UNQUENCHABLE PASSION

Beauty I was given at the time of my birth
—lamp and mirror of both of my arts—
as trustworthy model of my vocation.

—MICHELANGELO, SONNET 164

J ust a few hours before daybreak, in a stone house on the hills east of Florence, a man dipped his **quill** in ink and wrote by candlelight, "A male child was born to me." It was March 6, 1475.

Lodovico Buonarroti must have put down his quill with a feeling of relief. The child was healthy, and it was a boy—a good thing for a father who, under financial pressure, had been forced to accept a low-paying job as temporary government administrator of a small and remote area (Caprese and nearby Chiusi). In 15th-century Italy, boys had brighter prospects for earning an income than girls.

✠ Michelangelo's birthplace in the small town of Caprese, Italy. Maria Luisa Battistini

Lodovico's relief might have been expressed in the child's name—Michelangelo. It was not, following tradition, a name passed down through generations. It had been chosen with care, maybe as a prayer or a fulfillment of a vow to the Archangel Michael, a great heavenly warrior according to Christian beliefs.

Breathing Marble

WHEN LODOVICO'S temporary job was about to end, he prepared to return to his native Florence, one of Italy's most culturally and economically important cities. At 31 years of age, he still hoped his financial situation would improve. The prospects were dim. His family, once prominent and successful, had been in decline for decades.

As part of his moving arrangements, he traveled to Settignano, a small town three miles from Florence, in an area rich with olive trees and vineyards. There, he owned a villa and a little farm producing grains, meat, eggs, figs, wine, and olive oil—a source of moderate but steady income. One purpose of his visit was to hire a woman who could take care of Michelangelo.

Hiring a **wet nurse** for the time-consuming task of breastfeeding and caring for an infant was very common in Lodovico's day, especially for well-to-do families. In Lodovico's case, it also gave his young wife, Francesca de' Neri, a chance to rest after giving birth. Their oldest son, Leonardo, was only 16 months, and Lodovico was hoping to have more children. At a time of frequent wars and violent uprisings, when many died before the age of five and

+ 16th-Century Italy

contagious diseases wiped out entire towns, children were a source of security. Sons could work hard, defend the family and its properties, and provide for their parents. Daughters could marry into good families and create a network of support and protection.

Michelangelo was too young to understand what was happening when his parents left him with a wet nurse in Settignano. As the months went by, he probably grew close to his nurse, who came from a family of **stonemasons** and had married a stonemason. In fact, almost every man in Settignano was busy working stone. The town's **quarry** produced a very popular gray stone called *pietra serena* ("serene stone"), which had been used for centuries for some of the most important buildings in Florence.

Later in life, Michelangelo thought this early environment had inspired his great love for sculpture. Following a popular belief, he believed "the milk of the **foster-mother** has such power in us that often it will change the disposition." In any case, in Settignano he might have learned to appreciate the feel and appearance of the finest stone.

✤ Italian Pronunciation ✤

Many people find Italian pronunciation easier than English because it works with fixed rules.

The vowels have fairly set sounds.

a is always pronounced as the *a* in *father*
e can be pronounced either as the *e* in *let* or as the *a* in *late*
i is always pronounced as the *i* in *marine*
o can be pronounced either as the *o* in *soft* or as the *o* in *sold*
u is always pronounced as the *u* in *rule*

Most consonants are pronounced as they are in English. These are some exceptions:

h is always silent
when *c* is followed by an *e* or an *i*, it is pronounced *ch* as in *cheese*
when *g* is followed by an *e* or an *i*, it is pronounced *j* as in *job*
when *sc* is followed by an *e* or an *i*, it is pronounced *sh* as in *shame*
ch is pronounced as a *k*
gh is pronounced *g* as in *game*
gn sounds like the first *n* in *onion*
gli sounds like the *lli* in *million*

That's why the *ch* in *Michelangelo* sounds like a *k*, and the *c* in *Medici* sounds like an English *ch*.

Growing Up in Florence

IN THE spring of 1478, by the age of three, Michelangelo was back with his parents in Florence. It was at that time that the city ruler, Lorenzo de' Medici, was almost killed in a rebellion that took the life of his brother and coruler Giuliano. Filled with fury, Lorenzo ordered that the main culprits be beaten and then hanged from the windows of his palace for all to see. Others were brutally killed as well, and their families exiled. At the end of his life, Michelangelo still

remembered witnessing this awful scene as his father carried him around town.

Even in peaceful times, however, life for the Buonarroti was not easy. Lodovico kept getting deeper in debt. Unable to get other government jobs, he and his family had to stay in a small, dim house near the majestic church of Santa Croce, living off the small proceeds of his farm in Settignano. A few blocks north of the house stood the dreary brick walls of the debtors' prison, with four guard towers looming above them. To Lodovico, it was a constant reminder to keep his debts in check.

As was common at that time, Lodovico shared the home with his aged mother, his brother, and his sister-in-law. Extended family units were convenient, as each person could help and protect the others. In the meantime, his immediate family was growing. After Buonarroto, Francesca had two more sons, Giovan Simone and Gismondo. The arrival of Gismondo marked a time of both joy and deep sorrow. Like many mothers in those days of limited medical resources, Francesca died while giving birth, leaving Lodovico alone to care for his five boys. Michelangelo was only six years old.

Out of the Classroom

IN SPITE of his financial woes, Lodovico strove to uphold the memory and maintain the respectability of the Buonarroti name. He taught his sons to be proud of the family's coat of arms—blue with two golden diagonal stripes—and told them fascinating stories of their ancient lineage, which extended back to the medieval counts of Canossa, an illustrious family related to the head of the Holy Roman Empire. This story—quite certainly a legend—was very dear to Michelangelo, who made frequent mention of his lineage and imperial blood later in life.

✝ A modern-day view of Florence from Settignano. Anonymous, with permission

Lodovico tried to direct his sons to a lucrative and esteemed trade as cloth merchants or money changers, traditional professions in his family. Noticing Michelangelo's quick intelligence and exceptional memory, he sent him to grammar school at about eight years old. To his dismay, he discovered the boy was not very interested in his studies. In spite of his father's rebukes and even beatings (a more accepted form of discipline at that time), Michelangelo preferred to spend his time drawing—on countless sheets of paper and even on walls—or watching artists at work.

It was the Renaissance—an exciting period of renewal and discovery in every aspect of human learning and expression. Filled with busy workshops and famous artists who competed with each other, Florence was the best place in Europe for art lovers.

Michelangelo might have passed some of these workshops on his way to and from school, or when he ventured to other areas. Florence,

❧ Art and Sculpture in the Italian Renaissance ❧

The word *renaissance* means "rebirth." The Renaissance usually describes the period between the 14th and 16th centuries—a time marked by a desire to rediscover Greek and Roman works of art and literature, as well as to find new ways of expression. It is considered the greatest flowering of the arts in history.

During the Middle Ages (the time between the Roman Empire and the Renaissance), art was meant to portray ideas rather than real life. People were depicted in stiff, emotionless poses, with their feet off the ground, and scenery and nature were not considered relevant. Size was used to mark importance rather than perspective. For example, an important man would be portrayed in a larger size than other figures, even if he was farther away.

In the Renaissance, artists paid more attention to details and began to represent human figures in natural poses and realistic settings. They studied human proportions carefully, even dissecting dead bodies to understand the position of muscles, ligaments (connective tissues), and bones. Natural sceneries also became more important.

Renaissance sculptors went beyond the predominant style of the Middle Ages (bas-relief), which stood out only partially from the walls to which it was connected, and returned more frequently to the three-dimensional forms produced by the ancient Greeks and Romans.

In spite of the names given to these time periods (the Middle Ages have also been called the Dark Ages), medieval art and sculpture has its own special beauty and meaning. Today both the Middle Ages and the Renaissance are appreciated for their artistic and literary value and for their contributions to our culture and thought.

while a bustling city, was relatively small and could be walked across in less than an hour. So Michelangelo could easily visit not only his local church of Santa Croce, to gaze on the work of famous artists such as Giotto and Donatello, but also other churches, like Santa Maria del Carmine, which housed paintings by Masaccio. All these artists had a great influence on young Michelangelo's art.

He often visited these churches with friends who had an equal passion for art. His closest friend was Francesco Granacci, a young man five years older than him, who had already worked in a few workshops. When Michelangelo met him, Francesco was an apprentice for one of the most popular and renowned Florentine artists, Domenico Ghirlandaio. To young Michelangelo, Francesco must have been an exciting role model.

Francesco and Michelangelo were different in many ways. The older boy was handsome and well built, so much so that he had been chosen as a model for a famous painting displayed in a local chapel. Michelangelo was thin and delicate and looked almost sickly or undernourished. Francesco was from a simple family of small merchants who sold mattresses and used furniture, while Michelangelo's father, even in the midst of his financial distress, emphasized his noble lineage and maintained a disdain for humble occupations. In spite of these differences, the boys became good friends.

When Francesco understood Michelangelo's passion for art, he gave him some drawings to copy. Stunned by the young boy's abilities, he then took him to Ghirlandaio's workshop and introduced him to the artist. For Michelangelo, it was a dream come true.

Excitement in the Workshop

AN ARTIST'S life was not what Lodovico had envisioned for his son. As much as people appreciated art, artists were still considered simple workers. Until then, for example, there had been little or no distinction between sculptors, masons, and stonecutters, and Lodovico didn't

✝ **Woodcut of 16th-century Florence.**
From the Nuremberg Chronicle, Michael Wolgemut, Wilhelm Pleydenwurff
(Text Hartmann Schedel), licensed under public domain via Wikimedia Commons

ACTIVITY CREATE A MONSTER

+ An early painting by Michelangelo, based on the engraving *The Temptation of St. Anthony* by Martin Schongauer. Kimbell Art Museum, Fort Worth, Texas / Art Resource, NY

FRANCESCO SHOWED Michelangelo a drawing of St. Anthony attacked by temptations (which took the form of monsters) and encouraged him to reproduce it in color. Michelangelo went to the fish market to study shapes and colors. Create a fearsome monster by using objects you find in nature.

Materials

+ Several objects from nature, or from your local grocery store, with shapes, colors, and textures fitting for a monster (fish, shrimps, pinecones, pineapples, horse chestnuts, celery root, etc.)
+ Paper
+ Pencil
+ Colored pencils, crayons, markers, or paints

1. Study the objects you have found. Think about what might make good, unusual, or frightening body parts and features, such as the torso, legs, eyes, hair, and so on.

2. Draw and color your special monster, copying your objects' shapes and colors.

want his son to be a lowly laborer. Michelangelo, however, was a very strong-willed child, and nothing would change his mind. In the end, Lodovico consented to let him join the workshop as an apprentice.

Besides, the family's financial situation made the small additional income appealing. By 1487, Michelangelo was already earning a small pay. The next year, his father signed a three-year contract allowing him to work for Ghirlandaio at an increasing rate of pay.

Apprentices learned to paint by working for their masters. They started out, at the age of seven or eight, with humble tasks—preparing the tools, grinding colors, and cleaning up after others. When they became fully familiar with the materials and the methods, they were allowed to help in more creative ways—preparing surfaces and painting small portions of the background. It was hard work, lasting 10 to 12 hours a day. Only after six or seven years of apprenticeship did young people start to work more independently.

Michelangelo's experience was somewhat different. He entered the workshop later than usual, was allowed to progress very quickly, and had plenty of time to study and copy the works of great masters, even outside the workshop. He also received a stipend soon after he started working, while many other apprentices paid their masters for the education they received. One of the reasons for this special treatment might have been Lodovico's influence as a member of a noble Florentine family.

Probably Michelangelo helped Ghirlandaio with the large **fresco** paintings in the best renowned church in Florence—Santa Maria Novella. There, he learned valuable lessons on how to master the difficult fresco technique and how to build the **scaffolds** that supported the artists and their materials.

Ghirlandaio soon noticed Michelangelo's extraordinary talents. He also discovered the young man's boldness and impertinence when, after giving his apprentices some of his own sketches to copy, he noticed Michelangelo had corrected them with bold, thick strokes. Many years later, Michelangelo smiled when his friend and biographer Giorgio Vasari showed him one of the same edited drawings. He "recognized it and was pleased to see it again, saying modestly that he knew more of the art when he was a boy than he did at that time, when he was an old man," Vasari explained.

On another occasion, Michelangelo copied with precision a drawing by a skilled artist, aged the paper with smoke, and gave it to the owner of the drawing, who realized it was a copy only when he saw the boy laughing with his friends. It's no wonder that Ghirlandaio never allowed Michelangelo to borrow his sketchbook.

Michelangelo interpreted the master's denial as an expression of envy. Years later, he told his biographer Condivi that Ghirlandaio

AS AN APPRENTICE, Michelangelo had to learn to make paint by grinding or crushing natural objects like stones, bark, insects, berries, flowers, and seashells. He then mixed them individually with a little portion of egg yolk to make the paint stronger. You can imitate this technique at home.

Materials

✢ 1 egg

✢ Paper towel

✢ Paper or plastic plate (or plastic sectioned palette)

✢ 1 teaspoon each of natural food coloring powders (for example, turmeric for yellow, paprika for red, cocoa for brown, charcoal for black) *or* colored chalk with mortar and pestle or plate and cup for grinding

✢ Paintbrushes

✢ Cup of water for rinsing the paintbrushes

✢ A drawing you have made, or a page from a coloring book

1. Separate the yolk from the white of the egg. (Reserve the white if you want to "varnish" your art when you're done.)

2. Gently place the yolk on the paper towel to absorb any remaining egg white.

3. Transfer the yolk to the middle of the plate (or palette).

4. Put a teaspoonful of each of the coloring powders around the yolk (making sure they don't touch it). If you are using colored chalk, grind the chalk first with a mortar and pestle or with the bottom of a strong cup or jar against a plate. You can also use a mortar and pestle to grind green leaves or flowers.

5. With a paintbrush, take a little yolk and mix it well with one of the powders. Keep stirring until you obtain a uniform color. Use a drop of water if needed.

6. Use the mixture to color a portion of your picture.

7. Continue creating colors and painting until your picture is colored. You can also mix colors to create new shades.

8. For a shinier effect, let the picture dry and then paint over it quickly with the egg white.

MICHELANGELO IMPRESSED Ghirlandaio with his **cross-hatching** skills, which he used to create shadows. Cross-hatching is a technique of shading by drawing lines that intersect—or cross—each other.

Materials

+ Paper
+ Pencil or colored pencils

1. Study Michelangelo's drawing in the picture at left. Do you see how he created the shadows by drawing many intersecting lines?

2. Now draw a circle. Decide where the shadows should fall. (If the light comes from the right, the shadows should be on the left side, and vice versa.)

3. Add shadows with a cross-hatching technique. Start by drawing many short parallel lines, close to each other, on one side of your circle, following the curve. The shadows will be in the shape of a crescent moon.

4. Turn the paper and draw more parallel lines on top of the others, going in a different direction from the first set of lines. Don't cover the first lines completely. You can leave some lines uncrossed in the middle.

5. Turn the paper again and draw more parallel lines on top of the others, going in a third direction. Again, don't cover the other lines completely. Try to stay close to the edge. This will turn your circle into a three-dimensional ball.

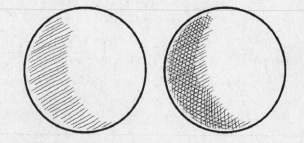

+ Michelangelo's cross-hatching technique can be seen in this drawing, copied from the painting *The Tribute Money* by Masaccio.
Foto Marburg / Art Resource, NY

"gave him no help whatever." In reality, he learned from Ghirlandaio much more than the simple foundations of fresco painting. His drawings show he had successfully adopted some of Ghirlandaio's techniques, especially his method of simplifying sketches by reducing them to geometrical patterns and his method of cross-hatching. On the other hand, they also show that Michelangelo surpassed his master. He drew more powerful and specific lines, and his drawings look more real.

In the Ruler's Palace

IN 1490, probably on request of Lorenzo de' Medici, Ghirlandaio allowed Michelangelo to attend the Garden of San Marco, a restricted area by the Medici Palace hosting a collection of antique statues and paintings. The curator of the area, Bertoldo di Giovanni, was an experienced sculptor who patiently taught a group of promising young artists the secrets of the trade. Michelangelo was fascinated. His brown eyes, shining with flecks of yellow and blue, surveyed the incalculable opportunities around him. Immediately, he spotted the best students and challenged himself to surpass them.

After receiving permission to study daily in the garden, Michelangelo never returned to the workshop. Given the young man's independent and brazen spirit, Ghirlandaio probably consented to his departure with some measure of relief.

Even this turn of events might be due to the influence of Lodovico, who was a distant cousin of Lorenzo. In those days, family ties, even if distant, were extremely important. In spite of his contempt for artistic professions, Lodovico must have been happy when Lorenzo offered the 15-year-old boy a generous salary and a place at his table as resident artist.

Family ties, however, can't make up for lack of talent, and Michelangelo's talent was truly impressive. According to his early biographers, what caught Lorenzo's attention was a copy of an ancient head of a laughing faun, a mythical figure that was half human and half goat. Lorenzo admired Michelangelo's rendition but chided him by asking why the old-looking faun still had all his teeth.

"Surely you should have known that old folks never have all their teeth, and that some are always wanting," he remarked. The comment was a sore stab to the boy's pride. The short wait for Lorenzo to leave the room felt like a thousand years. Finally, Michelangelo took back his chisel and knocked out one of the faun's teeth. In fact, he carved it out so carefully that it looked like the faun had naturally lost it. Immediately impressed by the young man's skill and desire for excellence, Lorenzo called for Michelangelo's father, who in front of the powerful ruler could only reply, "Not only Michael Angelo, but all of us, with our lives and all our best faculties, are at the service of your Magnificence."

Whether this story, reported by Michelangelo's early biographers, is completely true or not, Lorenzo admired the young man and offered to help him and his family in any way he could. This could have marked a change of fortune for the Buonarroti. Lodovico humbly asked only for a low-level, low-paying government position that had just become available. The position was long term and, however low paying, probably preferable to Lodovico over a better, short-term position. Lorenzo, however, interpreted this request as a lack of ambition. Smiling, he placed his hand on Lodovico's shoulder and said, "You will always be poor."

From the start of his residence in the Medici home, Michelangelo displayed a very personal and original sculpting style, daring to improve on the classics he was given to copy. He probably also learned how to model wax and clay for bronze casting, since that was Bertoldo's specialty. In one of his marble carvings, the *Battle of the Centaurs*, he used a chisel to make dramatic contrasts where more prudent artists

would have used a file. With the chisel, a small slip of the hand could cause irreparable damage, but Michelangelo was confident and bold. In fact, some of the marks in the marble suggest he may have been carving with both hands.

He also received a thorough education, since the Medici household was attended by some of the greatest minds of his time. For example, Angelo Poliziano, a well-respected scholar and poet, encouraged Michelangelo's love for poetry and probably suggested the theme of the *Battle of the Centaurs*. He might have also assisted the boy in his study of *The Divine Comedy*, the best-known work of 13th-century poet Dante Alighieri. Apparently Michelangelo had such a great memory that he could quote all three books of the *Comedy*. He also started to write short poems around this time.

Lorenzo continued to show great interest in Michelangelo and joined others in singing his praises. This attention, coupled with the teenager's habit of boasting, fostered envy and resentment in other resident artists. This friction resulted in a fistfight between Michelangelo and Pietro Torrigiano, a young sculptor renowned for his good looks and his fierce gaze. The two had known each other for some time. In fact, they used to visit a church together to study Masaccio's masterpieces.

As in every argument, there are two sides of the story. Michelangelo's early biographers said Torrigiano was jealous of him. Torrigiano, on the other hand, claimed Michelangelo was consistently provoking the others. "It was Buonarroti's habit to banter all who were drawing there," Torrigiano said. "One day, among others, when he was annoying me, I got more angry than usual, and clenching my fist, gave him such a blow on the nose, that I felt bone and cartilage go down like biscuit beneath my knuckles; and this mark of mine he will carry with him to the grave." The injury might have hurt Michelangelo's pride even more than his face. During the Renaissance, physical beauty was considered a very important quality as a mark of spiritual perfection.

Danger and Flight

On April 9, 1492, after battling some chronic and hereditary illnesses, Lorenzo de' Medici died. He was only 43. His rather unprepared 20-year-old son, Piero, took his place as head of the powerful family.

Distressed by the death of his **patron**, Michelangelo returned home. There, he found a different situation from when he had left. His father had remarried, and his older brother, Leonardo, had just left for Pisa to become a **friar**. Probably his younger brothers, all under 16 years old, didn't fully understand the impact Lorenzo's death was going to have on the future of Florence. For Michelangelo, it marked the end of one of the happiest periods of his life.

For many days, the young man lay around his house grieving. His teacher Bertoldo was dead, and Piero didn't seem too interested in continuing a fruitful relationship with his artists. Thankfully, Lodovico had retained his job and managed to support his family with his low income and the products of his farm. At the same time, he probably encouraged Michelangelo to look for better opportunities, since now he was the oldest son at home.

With the support of the **prior** of the church of Santo Spirito, Michelangelo invested some time in a serious study of **anatomy**. In those days, anatomy was learned by dissecting dead bodies, usually of criminals or prostitutes, who were presumed to be headed for hell. The prior allowed Michelangelo to work in the hospital, which was connected to the church.

Dissecting bodies was a very gruesome task, but Michelangelo believed it was necessary to understand the muscular structure of the body so he could reproduce it in his drawings and sculptures. He finally gave up, because those dissections "turned his stomach so that he could neither eat nor drink with benefit." By that time, however, he had learned enough.

As a gift to the prior, he carved a life-size crucifix out of soft poplar wood and painted in flesh tones. This is the only known work he ever carved in wood. In 1964, someone found a crucifix in the same church. Many think it's the one Michelangelo carved, even if the Jesus

✝ **Piero de' Medici, known as Piero the Fatuous (vain or foolish).** Erich Lessing / Art Resource, NY

FROZEN SCULPTURE

MOST LIKELY, Michelangelo used some carving instruments to make his statue of snow, but you can enjoy the thrill of making an ice sculpture without causing any danger to your hands.

Materials

+ Several balloons of different sizes and shapes
+ Food coloring of various colors (optional)
+ Water
+ Water faucet
+ Funnel (optional)
+ Ribbon
+ Freezer
+ Butter knife
+ Paper towels
+ Large tray

1. Stretch the opening of a balloon. If you want your sculpture to be in color, put a few drops of food coloring into the opening.

2. Fit the opening of the balloon tightly around the spout of a faucet and slowly fill it with water. You can also pour water into the balloon from a cup or bottle using a funnel, as long as the balloon can fit tightly around the stem. Fill the balloon as much as you like, but leave enough room to tie it. If you are planning to shape the balloon, leave additional room for that.

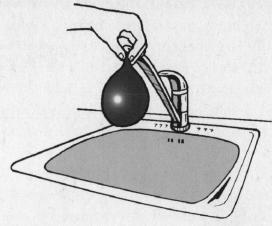

3. Tie the balloon. Repeat steps 1–3 with several balloons.

4. Press some of the balloons to create different shapes, and keep them pressed by placing a light weight on top or by loosely tying a ribbon around them.

5. Place them in a freezer (or outside on a cold winter day) until frozen. The time will depend on the size of your balloon. A small balloon will freeze in about three hours.

6. Once the water in the balloons is frozen solid, gently roll the edge of a butter knife on each balloon to break the coating, which will peel off

easily. You might want to hold the balloons with a paper towel while you work, because they will be very cold.

7. Arrange your sculptures on a large tray any way you like. For example, small, colored pieces can be made to look like fruit. If your tray is slippery, place a piece of paper towel under each piece to hold it in place.

8. On a winter day, you can leave the ice sculptures outside to beautify your yard. Otherwise, you may find a little room in your freezer to keep them for a while. Eventually, like Michelangelo's statue, your masterpieces will melt, but you can take a picture to remember them and show them to your friends (something he could not do).

figure portrayed on it—thin and drooping, with flabby muscles—is different from most of Michelangelo's sculptures, and doesn't seem to reflect his recent anatomical studies. The artist, however, might have been experimenting with different ideas and styles.

The only known serious commission Michelangelo received from Piero at this time was an eight-foot-tall marble statue of Hercules, a powerful hero from Greek **mythology**, long recognized as the symbol of Florence's independence. Later in life, the artist said he had carved the statue of his own initiative. He probably said that because Piero never paid him. The statue is now lost.

Sometimes called "the Fatuous" (vain), Piero displayed his immaturity in the winter of 1494 when, after an especially heavy snowfall, while extreme weather conditions were claiming many lives, he asked Michelangelo to build him a statue out of snow. Normally, at that time, children built snow lions (just like today we build snowmen), so that might have been what Michelangelo built.

Naturally, the young artist didn't want to invest his talents in a work that would disappear at the first warm rays of sunshine, but he wanted to keep good relations with Piero and was probably hoping to get paid for his previous work. As the temperatures remained low for eight days, the people of Florence were able to admire one of the shortest-lived masterpieces ever made. From that time on, Michelangelo returned to be part of the Medici household.

Soon, Piero's immaturity and inability to rule led Florence to the brink of collapse. From the north, a strong and well-armed French army threatened to attack the weakened city. Piero wavered in his decisions until, overtaken by panic, he joined the French leaders in a secret meeting where he made some unwise concessions. The people of Florence were ready to start a revolt.

By that time, a friar named Girolamo Savonarola had already been turning many Florentines against their government. In his powerful and vivid sermons, he had repeatedly warned them that the Medici's sins of greed and immorality were going to meet the impending judgments of God. As a deeply religious person, Michelangelo was very troubled by those frightening messages. Besides, his close ties to the Medici represented a potential threat in an angry town.

His fears were compounded by the recurring dream that plagued one of his dearest friends: a vision of the now dead Lorenzo de' Medici, barely covered by a torn black robe, warned Piero of his imminent and permanent exile. While Piero sneered at the warning, Michelangelo and two friends took it seriously. On an early October day, they rode their horses out of town without notifying Piero of their decision.

✛ Girolamo Savonarola.

✦ FROM ✦ FORGER *to* WONDER

From what you tell me, you have made possible the impossible.

—LODOVICO BUONARROTI, LETTER TO MICHELANGELO, 1500

A New Patron

The news of Michelangelo's departure spread quickly, most likely upsetting Piero's pride. At first, the artist and his friends traveled northeast, to the prosperous and renowned merchant city of Venice. Not finding whatever it was they wanted, after only one week they journeyed halfway back to Bologna, home of one of the oldest universities in the world.

Bologna's city doors were under a strict system of surveillance. All visitors were supposed to have their thumbnail stamped with a red wax seal. Somehow, Michelangelo and his friends entered the city without the stamp and were arrested. Unable to pay the fine, they were bound for prison.

The situation turned for the better when a nobleman who was present at the scene, Giovan Francesco Aldrovandi, took interest in Michelangelo. The artist had likely left Florence with letters of recommendation—a common practice by anyone seeking employment—and was able to show them to Aldrovandi, who was looking for a good sculptor. After ensuring the young men's freedom, he invited Michelangelo to stay at his house.

Michelangelo gave his friends what little money he had left and started a new chapter of his life in Aldrovandi's home. His assignment was to complete the tomb of Saint Dominic, who had died in Bologna. He only had to sculpt three small statues. The pay was satisfactory, and there was no time restriction.

Aldrovandi enjoyed Michelangelo's company. A lover of classical **Tuscan** authors (such as Dante Alighieri, Petrarch, and Boccaccio), Michelangelo took this opportunity to ask the Tuscan artist to read their works to him every night in their native accent.

Some other artists in town were jealous of Michelangelo's comfortable arrangement with Aldrovandi, especially one man who claimed Michelangelo's job had been offered to him first. In some ways, their jealousy is understandable, as this newcomer had rather effortlessly received a good commission, free material, and a privileged place to stay. Feeling threatened and perhaps unchallenged creatively and homesick,

Michelangelo returned to Florence soon after his commission was completed.

Michelangelo the Forger

FLORENCE HAD changed drastically in just over one year. Less than a month after Michelangelo's escape, the people of Florence had become frustrated by Piero's disastrous political decisions and expelled him from the city, together with most of the Medici family. By the time Michelangelo returned, Savonarola, without holding a formal political position, was exercising a much stronger influence on the citizens and had been able to impose strict rules on their behavior.

Although Michelangelo admired Savonarola, he was worried about the friar's teachings about art. Convinced that the arts of ancient Greece and Rome—with their nudes and their emphasis on human achievements and pride—could have a negative influence on Christians, the monk stirred the people to destroy such works and any artwork they had inspired.

Artists received very few commissions. Michelangelo had saved a little money from his previous job, but it was not enough to meet his needs and to help his father to raise a family on a modest salary. Since his older brother, Leonardo, had become a friar, Michelangelo shared his father's responsibilities. Thankfully, he still had one patron in town, another Medici (also named Lorenzo) who had been able to stay in Florence because he favored a government ruled by the people.

After making a small statue for Lorenzo, Michelangelo had time to sculpt a sleeping **cupid** for his own amusement. Lorenzo was impressed. It looked like the work of one of the finest ancient sculptors. In fact, if someone aged it, it could easily pass as a valuable antique. Michelangelo liked the idea.

After staining the statue with natural products, the artist buried it underground for a few weeks, then sold it to an art dealer for 30 **ducats**, which was a good payment for a small work of art. (In those days, a skilled laborer—for example, a sculptor or a blacksmith—would earn about 50 ducats a year.) The buyer in turn sold the piece for 200 ducats to a wealthy art lover in Rome—Cardinal Raffaele Riario.

It didn't take long for Riario to discover the fraud. According to Michelangelo's early biographers, the cardinal returned the statue to the dealer and sent a messenger to Florence to find the sculptor who had deceived him. The messenger was probably Iacopo Galli, a nobleman who worked as Riario's trusted banker. Pretending to be a buyer, Galli asked Michelangelo about his previous work, and the artist listed the cupid among his accomplishments. At that point, Galli revealed the intent of his mission and the cardinal's desire to see the artist in Rome. Michelangelo was probably filled with apprehension but, armed with a letter of recommendation from his patron Lorenzo, complied with the request.

The Bacchus

IN 1496, Rome was less impressive than Florence, and very different from the rich and glorious imperial capital it used to be. As 21-year-old Michelangelo passed the city walls, he found large uninhabited regions used as grazing grounds for cows, sheep, and goats. The population—$\frac{1}{20}$ of what it had been under Emperor Augustus—was mostly concentrated in the center of town, where the ancient **aqueduct** still brought some fresh water. The Tiber River, running abundantly through the town, was heavily contaminated by sewage.

Some buildings were hard to miss—the Colosseum, the Forum, and the Pyramid of Cestius, which stood out as an unexpected sight. Michelangelo was very impressed by the Pantheon, one of the best preserved ancient Roman buildings, which had been converted into a Christian church. Later, he used it as a model for some of his works.

Most likely, however, the meeting with Riario was the main thing on Michelangelo's mind. At only 35 years old, Riario was already one of the richest and most influential men in Rome. At the time of Michelangelo's arrival, Riario was building for himself an impressive

CREATE AN "ANTIQUE" STATUE

MICHELANGELO'S CUPID was made of marble, but you can make a similar statue with clay. Just like Michelangelo, you can make your work look older than it really is.

Adult supervision required

Materials

✛ 4 ounces oven-bake modeling clay (enough to make two small figurines or a larger one)

✛ Cookie sheet

✛ Tin foil

✛ Oven

✛ Paintbrushes

✛ ¼ cup strong coffee, tea, cocoa, melted black licorice sticks, or diluted brown tempera (1 tablespoon tempera mixed with 2–3 tablespoons of water; Michelangelo probably used licorice juice)

✛ 1 tablespoon diluted green tempera (optional)

1. Shape the clay into anything you like—a person, an animal, a flower, a dish, etc.

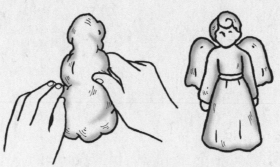

2. Line the cookie sheet with tin foil and place your figure(s) on the sheet. Bake according to the instructions on the clay box.

3. Allow your creations to cool completely. Then gently paint your brown coloring agent over them. You can paint less over some areas to mimic fading from the sunlight.

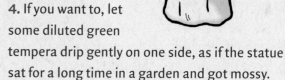
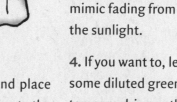

4. If you want to, let some diluted green tempera drip gently on one side, as if the statue sat for a long time in a garden and got mossy.

5. When the paint is completely dry, bake five more minutes to get a darker hue.

palace in the center of town. With his love for magnificence, arts, and antiquities, he personified the type of **clergy** Savonarola attacked in his sermons.

Michelangelo must have been surprised by Riario's welcoming response. Instead of condemning Michelangelo for his deceit, the cardinal, obviously impressed by his talent, provided the artist with a place to stay and invited him to admire his impressive art collection. The next day, Riario asked Michelangelo if he could sculpt something comparable to the items in his collection. Michelangelo agreed to do it, modestly warning the cardinal of his limited abilities.

In the end, Michelangelo produced a very original statue—a life-size image of Bacchus, the Roman god of wine. In most classic sculptures, Bacchus looked stable and dignified as god and master of wine. Michelangelo instead sculpted an inebriated young man whose eyes turn sideways, lost in his **intoxication**. At his feet, a childish **satyr**, a creature of Roman mythology, happily enjoys a bunch of grapes.

✛ **A 1493 map of Rome.**
Woodcut from Hartmann Schedel's *Weltchronik* (Nuremberg 1493), licensed under public domain via Wikimedia Commons, scanned by Aristeas

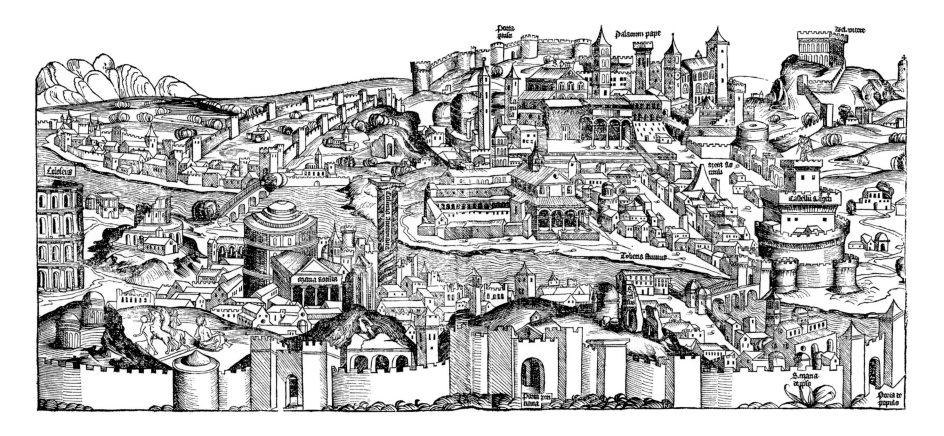

With his left hand, Bacchus carries a tiger skin—an animal traditionally considered sacred to the god. Michelangelo's biographer Condivi explained the skin as a symbol of the deadly effects of wine. With this statue, the artist might have tried to condemn the corruption and excesses of the Roman clergy and nobility.

In the end, Riario decided not to keep the statue, and sold it to Galli. A later drawing of Galli's garden shows the *Bacchus* without its right hand. Historians don't know when or how the statue broke. If it happened during the carving, either by mistake or due to a faulty piece of marble, Riario's rejection would have been easily justified. Another possibility is

✛ **A drawing of the *Bacchus* in the garden in the Casa Galli, by Maarten van Heemskerck.**
Kupferstichkabinett, Staatliche Museen, Berlin, Germany / Joerg P. Anders / Art Resource, NY

that Michelangelo intentionally mutilated the statue to make it look like an antique.

Hard Work and Preparation

MICHELANGELO REMAINED in Rome, but unlike most young artists, he didn't look for work in a local workshop. Riario had paid him 150 gold **florins**, an exceptional amount for a rather unknown sculptor. The florin was comparable to the ducat, so a sculptor normally made about 50 florins per year. As long as Michelangelo could make ends meet, he resolved to work independently.

He didn't have to wait long. In 1497, a powerful French cardinal, acting on Galli's recommendation, asked him to sculpt a statue of Mary, the mother of Jesus, holding her dead son's body—a common theme, known as **pietà** (Italian for "pity"). The cardinal wanted this statue as a decoration for his tomb, and offered to pay the hefty sum of 450 ducats. Michelangelo accepted.

Galli wrote up the contract and was so confident in Michelangelo's abilities that he made a daring promise: "It will be the most beautiful work of marble in Rome today, and no other living master will do better."

Michelangelo took the task seriously. To ensure the best results, he asked for an advance, bought a **dapple** gray horse, and traveled to the city of Carrara, about 300 miles north

STATUES IN MOTION

MICHELANGELO STUDIED ancient statues to learn the artists' techniques and to practice drawing different poses. He often imagined the same statues in other postures. You can use the same method.

Materials
✛ A photo of a statue
✛ Paper
✛ Pencil

1. Find a photo of a statue you like—perhaps one from this book, the Statue of Liberty, Rodin's *The Thinker*, a statue in your town, or the like.

2. For practice, sketch the statue on your paper as it looks in the photo.

3. Now try to envision the same statue in another position. For example, you might imagine what the Statue of Liberty would look like if the figure had both hands raised, one hand saluting, or whatever other poses you can think of. If the statue in your picture is missing one or more limbs, you can use your imagination to include the missing pieces.

4. Now make a new sketch, with your modifications. You can repeat this process as many times as you like to keep reimagining poses and practicing drawing.

If this activity is being done in class, compare your drawings and discuss your ideas with other students.

of Rome, to find a block of the finest marble, without cracks or discolorations. The Carrara quarry had been renowned throughout Europe since the days of the Roman Empire. Its white, pure marble was almost transparent.

Few artists ever went to quarries to choose their marble. Normally, they employed agents for the task. Michelangelo, however, didn't want to risk ruining this project by entrusting the responsibility to another person.

The process of obtaining marble was laborious and extremely dangerous. Michelangelo supervised the workers as they pounded iron or wood wedges in the mountain, causing the stone to split and fall. He assisted them in cleaning it, reducing it to the proper size, and dragging it down the mountainside with wooden sleds and ropes.

Before returning to Rome, Michelangelo stopped to visit his family for Christmas. The situation in Florence was tense. Seven months earlier, Pope Alexander VI, angered by Savonarola's attacks on the lifestyle of church leaders and by his political support of the French king, had **excommunicated** the friar. In open disobedience, Savonarola celebrated Christmas Day **mass** at the church of San Marco and led a solemn procession around the **piazza**.

Initially the **pope**, troubled by many serious problems, overlooked the offense. On February 11, 1498, however, Savonarola preached again, lashing out against the excesses of the pope and declaring him unfit for his office. A few days later, he started one of his frequent bonfires (known as bonfires of the vanities), where he encouraged people to burn any object that was considered vain, including works of art, jewelry, fancy clothes, and other decorative items. In the past, most Florentines had given him full support. This time, however, many expressed their disagreement by throwing trash in the fire. Savonarola was obviously on his way out. He was later arrested, tortured, and finally burned at the stake on May 23, 1498.

Michelangelo was already in Rome when Savonarola died, and must have been deeply affected by the events, although he never mentioned them specifically in his writings. In spite of some disagreements, he had admired the friar and had read his writings. In his old age, he admitted he had been "keeping always in his mind the memory of [Savonarola's] living voice."

Making the Impossible Possible

ACCORDING TO his contract, Michelangelo had one year to finish the pietà. In his eyes, however, the quest for perfection superseded any deadline. He worked thoroughly, paying careful attention to details—every strand of hair, each bone, muscle, vein, and drapery fold—and devoting months to polishing the statue until the stone reached its highest brilliance.

He had at least one helper, Piero d'Argenta, an artist approximately his age who had been working with him for a while. Besides lending a hand to the artistic work, Piero took care of many practical matters, such as paying bills and buying supplies.

Sculpting was hard work. This is one reason why, in Michelangelo's day, it was often equated with menial labor rather than art. It also requires much accuracy, because once some stone is chiseled away, it cannot be put back. Mistakes can't be erased, and it's very difficult to mask them.

Michelangelo worked mainly with a wide-headed mallet and three chisels—a heavy, pointed iron tool (called a *subbia*) for the preliminary work, a shorter-bladed tool (*calcagnuolo*) for most of the carving, and a claw-toothed chisel (*gradina*) to put on the finishing touches. To polish the statue, he used common materials such as pumice stone, sand, leather, and straw.

In 1499, the completed statue was hailed as a masterpiece. Vasari wrote that Michelangelo, hearing that the statue had been attributed to another artist, carved his name on it in the secrecy of night. In reality, since the name is carved on an otherwise pointless sash across Mary's chest, Michelangelo might have intended to put it there from the start, to signal to the world what he was capable of. Signing

❧ What Leonardo da Vinci Thought of Sculptors ❧

Leonardo da Vinci was a great artist of the Renaissance. Michelangelo often saw him as a rival. In his *Treatise on Painting*, Leonardo explained the difference between sculptors and painters, in his opinion.

Between painting and sculpture, I see only this difference: the sculptor works with greater bodily efforts, and the painter with greater mental efforts. This is clear because the sculptor works by the strength of his arms and by percussion, consuming the marble or other type of stone that encloses the subject, and he does it in a very mechanical way, often with much sweat, which, mixed with the powder, turns into mud, plastering his face. He is powdered all over by marble dust, which makes him look like a baker, and is covered by small chips of marble, as if he were coated with snow. His house is messy, dusty, and full of stone chips. For the painter, the opposite is true (if we talk about excellent painters and sculptors). The painter sits very comfortably in front of his work, well dressed, and moves his most light brush dipped in lovely colors. He dresses as he likes, and his house is clean, full of beautiful pictures and often filled with music or with the voices of readers of delightful works, which can be pleasantly heard without the clatter of hammers or other noises.

a sculpture had rarely been done before—and never in such a visible place—and it is something Michelangelo never did again.

The initial location for the *Pietà* (a chapel next to St. Peter's Basilica) no longer exists, and the statue is now showcased in a chapel inside the cathedral.

In Michelangelo's *Pietà*, Mary opens her arms to support her son's listless body, her expression graceful and accepting. Then, as

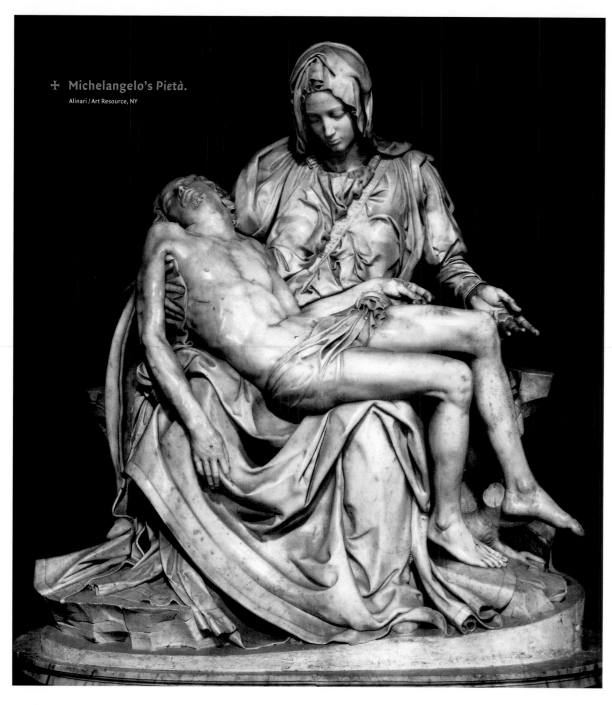

✝ **Michelangelo's *Pietà*.**
Alinari / Art Resource, NY

today, many believed this work embodied the ideals of beauty and perfection sought by Renaissance artists. Michelangelo was proud of his success and in a letter to his father said that he had "made possible the impossible."

His father was not entirely impressed. "I am very glad you are receiving honor," he said, "but it would be better if you had also some profit.... From what you write me, you don't have food. If you were at home, maybe you would have something and wouldn't have suffered so many discomforts, nor run into so many dangers; and honor would be worth more in your own country and at home."

Lodovico didn't know much about his son's artistic breakthrough and probably didn't fully understand it. He just knew that, in spite of the initial good payment, Michelangelo didn't have a steady income and was still living like a poor man.

He added some health tips. "Take special care of your head. Keep it moderately warm and don't ever wash yourself. Have a rub-down but don't wash." These instructions were common in both the Middle Ages and the Renaissance. Many thought washing left the pores open to illnesses. Michelangelo heeded the advice.

To earn a living, the artist accepted a painting commission but left the task halfway finished to accept a better job, offered by Cardinal Piccolomini (soon to be Pope Pius III)—the creation of 15 statues for a marble altar in the

Siena Cathedral. The abandoned painting assignment was the first of many unfinished commissions in Michelangelo's life.

The artist returned to Carrara to choose some marble, but after producing four of the 15 statues, he once again left the job unfinished to follow a more appealing opportunity.

The Giant

THE OPPORTUNITY arrived in 1501, when the council of Arte della Lana (Florence's wool **guild**, one of the most important corporations in the city) revived an idea of placing a statue of the biblical David on one of the **buttresses** of the city's cathedral, Santa Maria del Fiore. At that time, corporations commonly sponsored single works of art or the maintenance of important public buildings. In Florence, the wool guild was in charge of the cathedral's upkeep and beautification. Besides an adornment, the *David* was going to be an emblem of civic pride at a time when Florence was struggling to maintain its independence.

The main obstacle was the condition of the block of marble proposed by the council, which had been quarried about 40 years earlier. Time hardens marble, and exposure to the elements creates increasing damage. Besides, the block was already marred by tiny veins and holes, which contributed to its fragility, and it was so thin that a sculptor would have to keep the

⚜ The Republic of Florence ⚜

Normally, a **republic** is governed by a group of citizens elected by the people. Though Florence was called a republic, for 60 years (1434–1494) it was ruled by one family—the Medici. The Medici were not elected but passed on the power from father to son. Even if they kept the city's main governmental body (the *Signoria*, a council made up of eight elected men headed by a *gonfaloniere*), the Medici controlled the elections and influenced the council's decisions.

In some ways, the Medici rule was beneficial for Florence. Through the Medici's financial success in commerce and banking, Florence became known as "the cradle of the Renaissance." Under Lorenzo the Magnificent, the city enjoyed a large measure of peace and became the cultural center of Europe.

After the expulsion of the Medici in 1494, Florence was ruled by elected representatives. Besides the *Signoria* and a separate council of 12 elders, another council of 16 officials represented the different areas in Florence.

figure's limbs close to the body. These complications were compounded by the chisel marks made by at least one artist who had embraced and then abandoned the project.

Michelangelo applied for the job, making a wax model to show how a figure could be carved out of the block, which was quite slender in relation to its length (over 17 feet). This model, coupled with Michelangelo's recent accomplishments in Rome and his early statue of Hercules in Florence, convinced the council to assign him the job in spite of his having relatively little experience.

The contract gave Michelangelo two years "to make, carry out and perfectly finish this figure of man, so-called Giant." As for payment, he was treated as a salaried worker, with a pay of six florins a month. The total projected payment of 144 florins was a good sum for a young artist, considering that all his expenses were paid. Once again, Michelangelo was able to help support his family, soon becoming their sole provider.

Before this time, most images of David represented him as a young boy standing as victor on the head of the slain giant Goliath, the enemy of his people. Michelangelo wanted to create something more dynamic. He decided to capture the moment just before the final victory, when David focuses on the imminent and decisive throw, with one hand on the sling and one on the end of the strap. He also envisioned a more mature and confident David, as a powerful symbol of strength.

In the biblical account, David refuses to wear the king's armor. After killing the giant, he points out the contrast between the heavily armed Goliath and himself, who relied only on the power of God. Michelangelo took this idea further and, following the style of ancient sculptures, depicted David completely naked.

After hiring some masons to build a tall enclosure of wood and stone around the marble and a multilayered scaffold to reach every part of the stone, Michelangelo started to carve in

relative secrecy. He worked so rapidly that, by the end of February 1502, the council decided to give him a considerable raise, increasing his total earnings to 400 gold florins. It would have taken a skilled worker eight years to make the same amount of money.

Michelangelo dismantled the enclosure in 1503, when the work was almost finished. Vasari tells the story of a visit by Piero Soderini, the city's *gonfaloniere*. Apparently, Soderini was not completely satisfied with David's nose, thinking it was too large. Michelangelo obligingly mounted his scaffold, hiding a handful of marble dust in his hand. He then pretended to chisel away a portion of the nose, letting the dust fly into the air. In the end, Soderini expressed his satisfaction with the unchanged nose.

There is no confirmation that the story is true. In any case, Soderini and Michelangelo became good friends and held each other in high admiration, as Michelangelo became more and more committed to the ideal of the republic. In fact, Soderini was probably partially responsible for assigning the commission of the *David* to Michelangelo in the first place.

The statue was completed in April 1504. The deadline had been extended, partially because the city had asked Michelangelo to build a small bronze statue of David for a French diplomat. Michelangelo was not interested in this second project—especially since the diplomat wanted

✚ A bronze copy of the *David* overlooks Florence.
Maurizio

a copy of a statue by the famous sculptor Donatello—but agreed to do it because it was important for the newly formed Florentine Republic to maintain good relations with France.

By the time the *David* was completed, the Florentine government had decided, after many deliberations, to place it in Piazza della Signoria—Florence's main square, where the citizens gathered in times of both turmoil and triumph. Michelangelo was happy. It was exactly where he wanted it.

Moving the statue was not easy. It had to be suspended with strong ropes from a wooden framework mounted on a cart. The move started on May 14, 1504, at night, with torches lighting the way. Under the cart, 14 greased beams were constantly shifted as the cart moved forward at a snail's pace. The work required the effort of about 40 men, who pulled the cart and shifted the beams for four consecutive days. Each day, a large crowd gathered to watch. Michelangelo followed the move with vigilant eyes.

There were occasional problems. On the first night, some young men threw stones at the statue. No damage was done, and guards were placed around the *David* the following nights. Since the culprits belonged to families related to the Medici, they might have been protesting the symbol of the new republic.

After being placed on a pedestal, the *David* was finally revealed to the public. From various documents, it seems that the council had

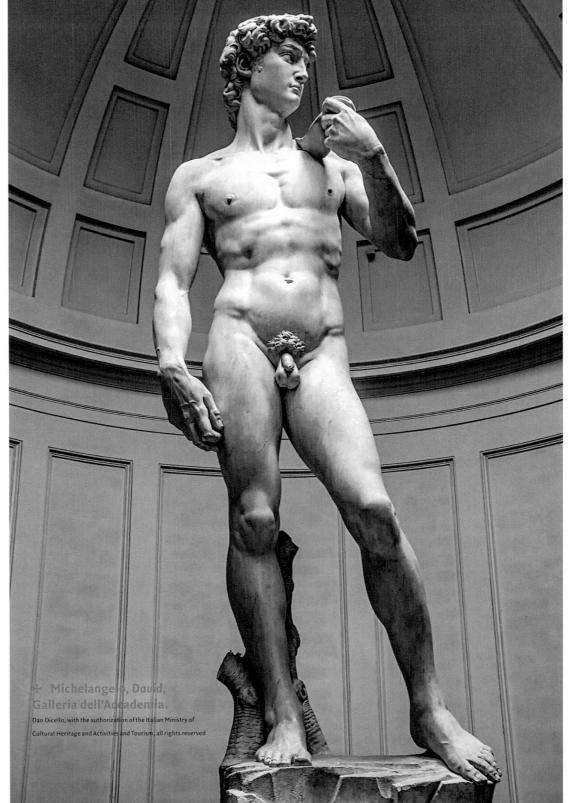

✦ Michelangelo, *David*, Galleria dell'Accademia.

hired some goldsmiths to create a garland to go around David's loins for a more modest appearance. They might have also placed a garland around his head.

The *David* gathered immediate praise and admiration. Viewers began to appreciate the details Michelangelo employed to give energy to the figure in spite of the limited width of the

THE MICHELANGELO CART

MOVE AN OBJECT across your room using the same method Michelangelo adopted to move the *David* across Florence.

Materials

✝ 3 empty paper towel rolls (or 3 long Lincoln Logs)

✝ Piece of strong cardboard or a thin book (8 inches by 10 inches or slightly larger)

✝ 1 unbreakable object (a small doll, stuffed animal, or figurine)

1. Lay the three rolls on the floor on one side of the room or at one end of a long table.

2. Plan your destination at the other side and make sure there are no obstacles on your way.

3. Put the cardboard on top of two rolls so that it rests on them firmly. Place the third roll in front of the cardboard. The three rolls should be spread evenly apart.

4. Place your object in the center of the cardboard.

5. Roll the board slowly, making sure the front part moves on top of the third roll.

6. As you keep rolling, the back roll will soon be free, so you can place it in front of the board.

7. Continue in this way until you reach your destination.

Does this feel like a slow, tedious way to move something? Imagine doing this with a heavy cart and large beams for four consecutive days!

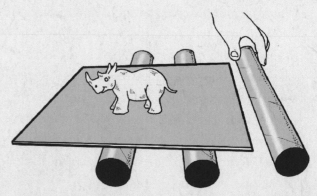

marble. For example, by turning David's head to the left and shifting the weight to his right leg, Michelangelo had suggested an imminent movement. This asymmetrical arrangement is part of a technique called **contrapposto** (counterpoise), which he had learned from studying ancient Greek statues.

Other important details are the intensity of David's gaze, his tense neck muscles, and the bulging veins on his right hand, all conveying a feeling of readiness and a sense of danger and anticipation.

Today, when photos of the *David* are taken close to the statue and directly in front of it, the head and the hands look disproportionately large. Most likely, Michelangelo wanted it this way to correct the effect of seeing the statue from below and from a distance—which is the way most people would have seen if it had been mounted, according to the original plans, on the cathedral's buttress.

In the 19th century, the *David* was placed inside the Accademia Gallery to protect it from the elements, while a copy replaced it in the piazza. A bronze copy was also positioned in Piazzale Michelangelo, overlooking the city—a popular spot for tourists who want to see a full view of Florence.

These measures, however, didn't protect the original *David* from the attack of a vandal who, in 1991, struck the statue with a hammer, much to the shock of nearby tourists. Thankfully, he was stopped before he could do too much damage, and he only managed to shatter the second toe of the left foot. Three tourists were stopped as they tried to leave the building with some fragments of the *David* in their pockets.

This was not the first injury the *David* sustained. In 1527, during an uprising, the *David* was hit by a flying bench, and one arm was broken in several pieces. After each incident, the statue was skillfully restored. Today, after warnings that earth tremors could damage the statue, the *David* rests on an earthquake-proof base and is constantly watched, filmed, and examined. It is both the most famous and the most monitored statue in the world.

✠ Michelangelo, *David*, Galleria dell'Accademia, detail.

✠ TO ✠
PLEASE *a* POPE

Nothing the greatest can conceive
That every marble block doth not confine.

—MICHELANGELO, SONNET 151

Many Irons in the Fire

As Michelangelo's fame spread throughout Florence and beyond, he began to receive new commissions. In 1503, even before he completed the *David*, the wool guild asked him to sculpt 12 marble statues of Jesus's **apostles** to decorate the Santa Maria del Fiore cathedral. It was a great opportunity, promising Michelangelo free material, free accommodations, and a long-term income. The sculptor began the work in 1506 with a statue of the apostle Saint Matthew.

Once again, he left the job incomplete in favor of a new commission. Still, the unfinished statue is very valuable, both as a work of art in its own right and as an example of his methods. Michelangelo's originality lies in his ability to sculpt as if he were freeing a figure imprisoned inside the marble. Vasari compared it to the way a body immersed in water is gradually revealed as the water is drained.

Later, Michelangelo expressed this same idea in a poem:

Nothing the greatest can conceive
That every marble block doth not confine
Within itself: and only its design
The hand that follows intellect can achieve

The commission that diverted Michelangelo from the *St. Matthew* was probably the decoration of a wall of the Great Council Hall in the main government building, the Palazzo della Signoria. The subject was a scene from the historic Battle of Cascina, which was fought in 1364 between Florence and Pisa and ended with Florence's surprising victory against all odds. The painting would have reminded the Florentines of their proud history, celebrating their newly independent republic.

Michelangelo was attracted to this project for different reasons. By then, he was deeply devoted to the cause of the newly instated republic. Also, the work had been commissioned by Piero Soderini, who had become a very good friend and allowed the artist the freedom, trust, and appreciation he craved.

Besides, Leonardo da Vinci, Florence's most acclaimed artist, had been commissioned to paint a different battle on a wall of the same hall, and Michelangelo, who saw Leonardo as a rival, was eager to compete with him.

Leonardo's commission was an intense scene of the 15th-century Battle of Anghiari between Florence and Milan. His design—a great tangle of bodies and horses—was immediately applauded for its originality and beauty.

Instead of competing with Leonardo by drawing another battle scene, Michelangelo chose a very unusual subject for a military painting—the moment just before the Battle of Cascina, when a sudden attack after a dull waiting period caught the Florentine army unprepared. In Michelangelo's drawing, 19 soldiers, who had escaped the oppressive heat by bathing in the Arno River, scrambled to shore. Michelangelo might have been trying to emphasize the need for alertness.

Leonardo began to have problems as soon as he started to paint. Having recently had a negative experience painting a fresco in Milan (*The Last Supper*), he decided to try a new technique that, unfortunately, caused the paint to drip. He tried to dry the walls by exposing them to a source of extreme heat, but the heat could not reach the highest parts of the painting. Discouraged by the mess, Leonardo abandoned the project.

Michelangelo didn't progress even as far as Leonardo. He produced a full-size drawing on paper, intending to transfer it to the wall, but before he could do so, he received an assignment he was unable to ignore. Pope Julius II summoned him to Rome to design and build a gigantic tomb. Soderini must have been disappointed, but the pope had extraordinary political powers in Europe, and Florence needed his favor.

In any case, Michelangelo's drawing and Leonardo's unfinished painting remained in the Council Hall, where they continued to attract many artists who were eager to copy them. Michelangelo's unique drawings depict a wide range of emotions simply by showing the subjects' expressive body movements.

In 1512, the Medici regained control of the city and turned the Council Hall into soldiers' barracks. Michelangelo's drawing, however, was put on display at the Medici Palace.

✦ **Portrait of Leonardo da Vinci with His Flying Machine by Emanuele Taglietti.** Emanuele Taglietti

LIKE MICHELANGELO, imagine there is a beautiful figure (a flower, a fruit, a fish, a duck, etc.) trapped in a block of raw material—in this case, a bar of soap. Try to carve it out, starting from the front and working your way into the bar.

Materials

✦ 1 bar of soap (Ivory is one of the softest)
✦ Clay modeling tool set (available at art and craft supply stores), or you can use what you have at home (such as toothpicks, brass fasteners, or a nail grooming kit)

1. Use the thinnest tool to draw an outline of your object on the soap.

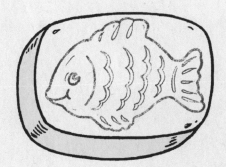

2. Use a larger tool to carve around the sides of your outline, as if you were extracting the object from the soap. You can smooth the edges and add some details as you go.

3. Start slowly and carefully chipping off the unused portion of the soap. If you are not sure if the soap will chip off easily, continue to dig deeper.

4. Once all the extra soap is chipped off, make your statue smoother and begin work on the details. Use the thinnest tool to add small lines.

35

Eventually, it was torn to pieces by overly fervent artists who took the fragments home to study them. Today, some of these other artists' copies are still available, as well as some of Michelangelo's earlier sketches.

Michelangelo's stay in Florence from 1501 to 1512 marked one of the most fruitful times of his life. Besides the works already mentioned, Michelangelo completed a few small commissions, including a statue of Mary and her child for the church of Notre Dame in Bruges, Belgium, and a painting (known as *Doni Tondo*) of the Holy Family—Joseph, Mary, and Jesus—commissioned by a friend.

The fact that he completed these and a few other works while leaving other commissions undone indicates that, by this time, he had already established his lifelong habit of giving priority to what he liked to do.

These works also show that, in spite of his outward scorn of Leonardo, Michelangelo strove to learn from him. This is especially evident in the *Doni Tondo*, where the combination of figures, the energy of the child being passed over Mary's shoulder, and the otherworldly background evoke similar paintings by Leonardo. Michelangelo's colors, however, are more brilliant, and the contrast between figures is more marked.

Another difference is that, while Leonardo's backgrounds tend to emphasize the beauty and peacefulness of nature, Michelangelo's is crowded by a group of naked figures. Most biographers agree that the young child dressed in animal skin who seems to be staring at Jesus is meant to be his cousin, the prophet John the Baptist, who in the Bible links the time before the birth of Jesus (symbolized by the naked figures in the background) to the Christian era.

✝ **Michelangelo's *Doni Tondo*, in its original frame at the Uffizi Gallery in Florence.**
Dan Dicello, with the authorization of the Italian Ministry of Cultural Heritage and Activities and Tourism

IN THE DAYS BEFORE PHOTOCOPIERS, fresco artists had to enlarge their drawings by hand so they could reproduce them on walls. In this activity, you'll learn how to accurately enlarge drawings by hand.

Materials
✛ 9-by-12-inch sheet of construction paper
✛ Pencil
✛ Ruler
✛ 12-by-16-inch sheet of construction paper
✛ Colored pencils, crayons, markers, or paints (optional)

1. Place the 9-by-12-inch piece of paper horizontally on your desk or table and draw a simple picture (for example, a house or a flower), making sure it covers most of the paper.

2. Using the ruler, measure out 3-inch sections along the edges of the paper and mark them with your pencil (three on the top and bottom, and two on each of the other sides).

3. Still using the ruler, connect the dots on the top edge with the corresponding dots on the bottom. Do the same with the dots on the two sides. Your paper will be divided into 12 squares. Put this paper aside for a while.

4. Place the 12-by-16-inch piece of paper horizontally on your desk or table.

5. Using the ruler, make 4-inch marks along each edge of the paper.

6. Connect the dots as you did for the first paper. If your ruler is too short, you may have to make more marks in the middle of the paper to help guide your ruler. You will end up with 12 squares again.

7. Now place the smaller paper in front of you as a model to copy. Look at one square at a time, and redraw your picture on the larger paper, using the grid as a guide. If it's easier, you can cover all the squares except the one you are trying to copy. Be patient. Think how much time Michelangelo had to invest in copying his sketches to large pieces of paper, before transferring them to the walls.

In the end, you should have a larger copy of your original drawing. If you want to, you can erase the grid lines and color the pictures.

You can also set this picture aside for another activity (see "Transfer a Picture" in chapter 4).

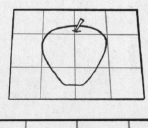

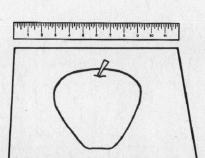

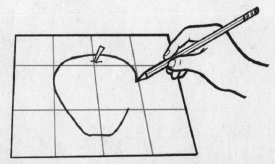

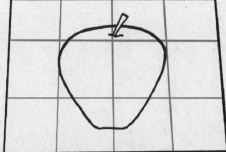

Plans for a Colossal Tomb

FOR BEING 60 years old, Julius was incredibly robust. Known as "the warrior pope," he liked to dress in silver armor while he led his troops in the expansion of papal territories or the subjugation of opposing towns. To Michelangelo, Julius revealed his grandiose vision of rebuilding Rome after the model of the ancient city.

For the time being, he wanted the sculptor to create a tomb of about 23 by 36 feet, decorated with 40 large statues and designed for his own burial. He was ready to invest at least 10,000 ducats. It would have been a modern wonder.

The project was rather unpractical, because there was no room in St. Peter's Basilica to fit such a structure. Even if the pope had made

changes to the church, the new tomb would have obscured the small tomb of St. Peter that was at the center. Still, Julius was not deterred. He believed he could solve these problems later.

The pope's magnificent vision and the enormous task at hand—which would have provided enough work for a lifetime—spurred Michelangelo into action. After receiving an advance payment of 1,000 ducats, he left for Carrara, where he stayed for about eight months with two helpers, a horse, and some food supplies. There, he worked alongside the locals, extracting more than 100 tons of pure white marble.

Once, while admiring the beauty of the Apuan Alps overlooking the sea, he envisioned himself carving a colossal statue right in the mountain. (Today, such a work could be

✛ **The Carrara quarries.**
Salvatore Petrantoni

compared to Mount Rushmore in the United States.) It would have been a landmark for sailors, even at a great distance. It was an extremely ambitious and unprecedented idea, but one that, to the artist's great regret, never came to fruition.

Michelangelo returned to Rome in January 1506, just in time to admire a new and astonishing archeological finding. It was the most famous discovery of his day—a statue of Laocoön, a mythical Trojan priest who angered a god by urging his fellow citizens not to accept the wooden horse the Greeks offered as a present. The god, who wanted a Greek victory, sent snakes to kill him and his sons. The statue had been described in classical writings, so it was already famous when it was found.

Michelangelo found great inspiration in the dying priest's contorted movement depicted in the statue. As soon as the marble arrived from Carrara, he tried to incorporate the same powerful feelings of anguish and passion in the pope's tomb, creating the statues of two slaves, one caught in the agony of death and another strained in an effort to find freedom from his chains. The posture of the second slave is particularly similar to Laocoön's. As in many other works, Michelangelo expressed his desire to experiment with new ideas and to apply new knowledge.

At the same time, Michelangelo's return to Rome was tinged with disappointment, as Julius seemed distracted with another glorious project—the reconstruction of St. Peter's Basilica. For this work, the pope had found a capable architect: Donato Bramante, who had already made a name for himself in Milan. On April 17, 1506, the first foundation stone for the new church was laid.

Bramante had a charming personality, and his plans for the cathedral left Julius obviously impressed. Michelangelo, on the other hand, became convinced that Bramante was actively trying to divert the pope's attention from the tomb so he could focus on the cathedral.

The day before Easter, as he attended a meal with the pope and his entourage, Michelangelo heard Julius say he had no intention of spending one more cent for any type of stone, big or small. Alarmed, the artist tried to talk to the pope but was told to come back later. His request continued to be denied daily, until he received clear orders to stop inquiring.

Highly humiliated and convinced he had wasted much time and effort on the tomb, Michelangelo left by horse in a fury, instructing his assistants to sell all the contents of his house.

A Collision of Wills

THE POPE sent five couriers to arrest Michelangelo, but by the time they reached him he was safe in Florentine territory. In a letter to the pope, he explained he had no intention

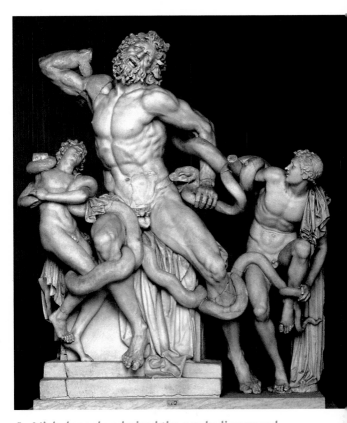

✛ Michelangelo admired the newly discovered *Laocoön*, a statue from about the first century CE.

SUGAR DECORATIONS

SCULPTURES MADE OF SUGAR were very fashionable on the tables of popes and noblemen. They were usually made by sculpting a block of sugar. In this activity, you learn an easier and safer way.

Adult supervision required

Materials

- ✛ Small pot
- ✛ ¼ cup water
- ✛ 3 tablespoons of honey
- ✛ 1 packet (.25 ounces) of unflavored gelatin
- ✛ Wooden spoon
- ✛ 1 pound confectioner's sugar
- ✛ Mixing bowl
- ✛ Cutting board
- ✛ Stove
- ✛ Whisk (optional)
- ✛ Food coloring (optional)
- ✛ Flavoring (optional)

1. Mix water and honey in a small pot and sprinkle the gelatin in the mixture, mixing well with a wooden spoon.

2. Pour most of the confectioner's sugar into a mixing bowl. Sprinkle some of the extra sugar on a cutting board.

3. Place the small pot on the stove over low heat. Keep stirring until the mixture is warm. Do not bring it to a boil.

4. Pour the mixture into the mixing bowl over the sugar, and combine the ingredients with a whisk or wooden spoon until it's too hard to stir.

5. Transfer the mixture to the cutting board.

6. Dust your hands with some of the sugar and knead the mixture until it's as soft as Play-Doh.

7. To color the dough, divide it into small balls. Flatten one ball, drop two drops of food coloring in the center, and fold it. Knead until the color is uniformly spread. If you find

that the food coloring made the dough too sticky, you can add a little more sugar. Create as many colors as you like. You can also knead a few drops of flavoring into your dough, such as maple extract or vanilla.

8. When you are done, mold and sculpt your dough into fun shapes, as you would shape Play-Doh.

9. Let your creations dry (about 10–15 minutes for very small items, such as flowers and hearts, or several days for large objects, such as a mug).

You can place small decorations around the dinner table to mark your guests' places, or use them to garnish a cake. Larger decorations can be used as centerpieces, or at place settings to surprise your guests when they discover they are edible!

of going back to Rome, because he had been treated unjustly. Since the pope didn't seem interested in finishing the tomb, Michelangelo felt he had no further obligation.

Later, in a letter to a close friend, he alluded to another reason for his departure—one he didn't want to mention explicitly. "It's enough to make me believe that, if I had remained in Rome, my tomb would have been built before the pope's." It is possible that his fears of Bramante's jealousy had degenerated into a terror of a secret plot against his life.

He ended the letter to Julius with a proposal: if the pope wanted him to finish the tomb, he could send the money to Florence, where Michelangelo could work "better and with more love" because he would have fewer worries.

The pope, however, had no intention of accepting this long-distance arrangement. Between July and August, he sent at least three letters to Soderini requesting his artist back. In November, when he insisted again, after having reconquered the city of Bologna, the Florentine government finally obliged.

By that time, Michelangelo's fears had run so wild that Soderini described him as "terrified." To ensure the artist was treated kindly, Soderini sent a letter addressed to his own brother, who was a cardinal in the pope's service.

"We can assure you that Michelangelo is a distinguished man, the first of his art in Italy, indeed perhaps of the whole world," he explained. "Kind words and gentle treatment can gain anything from him. It is only necessary to let him see that he is loved, and is favorably thought of, and he will produce astonishing works."

On the other hand, harsh manners might induce Michelangelo to run away. Soderini had in fact recently dissuaded Michelangelo from

✤ The Papacy ✤

After Jesus of Nazareth's death around 33 ce, his message spread and his followers gradually grew in number. To worship, they united in local communities administered by men known as elders or bishops. The word *pope* (from the Greek *pappas*, meaning "father") was traditionally used for all bishops. As time went by, bishops gained more responsibilities and often oversaw large areas. Some became more important than others. In the West, the most important bishop was the bishop of Rome, who later became known simply as pope.

Not all Christian churches recognize the pope of Rome as head of the universal church. The Eastern Orthodox Church, for example, is led by multiple "patriarchs," each from a different country where the religion is practiced, such as Russia, Serbia, and Bulgaria.

In Rome, popes gradually gained more spiritual, political, and economical power, which led to strong clashes with European rulers. The darkest time in the history of popes was in the 1300s, when the Roman Catholic pope was forced to move to Avignon, France, generating the rise of a second, and then a third pope, all claiming supremacy at the same time.

By the time Michelangelo moved to Rome, the papacy had returned to that city and was striving to strengthen both its spiritual and political authority.

accepting an invitation by Sultan Bayezid II to design a 1,000-foot-long bridge across the Bosporus strait, linking Europe and Asia.

Still fearful and reluctant, on November 21, 1506, Michelangelo rode into Bologna, escorted by some of Florence's highest officers. To a friend, he explained he was forced to go as though "with a rope around my neck."

After hearing mass at the San Petronio Basilica, Michelangelo was taken to see the pope, who exclaimed angrily, "You ought to have come to us, and you have waited for us to come to you!" He was referring to the fact that Bologna is much closer to Florence than to Rome.

Kneeling down, Michelangelo begged for forgiveness, explaining he had left because of the pain of being set aside. Apparently, the pope not only granted him forgiveness but also defended Michelangelo from a priest who tried to excuse the artist by describing all painters as ignorant.

"You are the ignorant one," the pope shouted, sending the priest out of the room. While this story might have been embellished, it is true that Julius displayed much respect for the sculptor. Michelangelo had already started to change the traditional relationship between patrons and artists, removing the conventional image of the artist as a simple and unlearned artisan.

Still silent about his tomb, Julius gave Michelangelo a new commission, this time in Bologna: a 14-foot bronze statue of himself, in commemoration of his regained territories. When he asked Michelangelo how much it would cost, the artist estimated 1,000 ducats, but he hastened to add that casting bronze was not his art and he was not sure it would turn out well.

"Go to work and keep casting it until you succeed," the pope replied, "and we will pay you to your satisfaction." He then gave official orders that the artist should not leave Bologna without his permission.

To create this massive image, Michelangelo asked for the assistance of his friend Piero d'Argenta and two other sculptors. The four shared a single bed in the artist's rented room. The two new sculptors, however, didn't last long—Michelangelo accused one of cheating.

The work presented many difficulties for a sculptor with limited experience with bronze. Michelangelo had to form a sculpture in **terracotta** clay, then bake it and coat it with a thick layer of wax. From this, he had to build a terracotta mold that was thick enough to stand the heat of molten bronze. Finally, he had to pour the bronze into the mold, making sure it reached every corner, expelling the melted wax through some prefabricated ducts.

His first attempt was a failure. Only the bottom half of the statue was cast correctly, and he had to repeat the whole process. In a letter to his brother Buonarroto, he described his hardship. "I live here in the greatest discomfort and extreme exhaustion, doing nothing but work day and night. I have undergone so much toil and so many hardships that, if I had to build another statue, I don't think I would survive." Besides, he disliked Bologna. He thought its citizens were envious, the city was dark, and the wine "as depressing as can be." The climate was also unbearable. "Since I have been here, it has rained only once, and we have suffered a heat I would have never believed possible."

In addition to these problems, after the pope returned to Rome, the Bolognese started to show their intolerance of his rule. "Here we are engulfed by armors," Michelangelo informed his brother Giovan Simone. "This whole place has been in arms for four days, with great noise and danger, especially for the church." The situation was also menacing for the artist who was building a monument to celebrate the papal conquest of the city.

Finally, however, Michelangelo saw the fruit of his labors and had the satisfaction of silencing those who had doubted his ability. "I think someone's prayers must have helped me and kept me in health," he wrote to Buonarroto, "because everyone in Bologna was of the opinion that I should never complete it."

The statue, placed in the main city square, depicted the seated pope with his right hand raised in benediction and his left hand holding the keys of St. Peter's.

Soon after the unveiling, Michelangelo borrowed a horse from a friend and left for Florence in haste. A few years later, the people of Bologna rebelled against the pope and destroyed Michelangelo's statue, recycled the bronze, and built a cannon, which they playfully named "the Julia."

✝ San Petronio Basilica in Bologna, Italy. Andrea Pierleoni

✛ A ✛
DAUNTING
CEILING

I am not a painter.

—MICHELANGELO

A New Challenge

In the spring of 1508, while Michelangelo was finally enjoying some peace and quiet, Pope Julius called him back to Rome, but not—as the artist was hoping—to finish the tomb. Instead, he asked Michelangelo to decorate the ceiling of the Sistine Chapel, in St. Peter's Basilica. After protesting that painting was not his strength, the artist conceded to the idea and made plans to achieve it.

The Sistine Chapel took its name from Pope Sixtus IV, who had it built and decorated with paintings by famous artists. It was one of the most important locations for the Roman Catholic Church. The assembly of cardinals met there to choose each new pope, and the most esteemed guests were taken there to attend mass.

In those days, church ceilings normally depicted a blue sky filled with stars, and the Sistine Chapel ceiling was no exception. Initially, the pope wanted Michelangelo to simply restore the previous painting, which had badly chipped, adding a pattern of circles and squares and images of the 12 apostles.

To Michelangelo, this plan was doomed to produce "a poor thing." If he was to be involved in this work, he wanted to do something magnificent. The pope agreed to let him do as he pleased. The artist's drawings show the progress of his thoughts, from the original plan to the astounding work we have today.

In the center of the ceiling, Michelangelo portrayed major events from the first chapters of the Bible: three scenes of the creation of the world, three scenes of the story of Adam and Eve, and three scenes of the story of Noah and the Great Flood.

Around these central scenes, he placed 12 panels with alternating portraits of biblical prophets and nonbiblical prophetesses (known as **sibyls**) who had predicted the coming of Jesus, as well as eight triangular scenes of biblical families. At the four corners, he added four depictions of biblical stories of salvation.

Around these, he designed 16 half-moon-shaped spaces depicting Jesus's ancestors. Of these, only 14 survive because he had to destroy two when he painted the Last Judgment on the altar wall. Most likely, he discussed all these plans with some of the pope's **theologians**.

Obstacles and Trials

IT WAS a tremendous undertaking. The ceiling was huge—about 13,000 square feet—and was curved. Also, the celebration of mass had to continue while the work took place. The scaffolding Michelangelo would use to reach the ceiling had to meet these challenges.

From the start, Michelangelo rejected Bramante's suggestion to hang a scaffold from the ceiling by ropes. After all, how could anyone go back and fill the holes left by the scaffold after the ceiling was painted?

Once again revealing strong engineering skills, Michelangelo designed a structure similar to a bowed bridge with a system of steps, stretching from one side of the chapel to the other. Today, the holes that supported the structure are still visible, but they are on the side walls and don't interfere with the painting.

As practical as it was, the structure allowed a very limited space in which to move. Michelangelo normally painted standing up, or sometimes kneeling, with his arms raised. Summers were especially hot because heat naturally rises. If the work continued through the evening, painting by candlelight generated even more heat.

| ACTIVITY | PILLAR POWER |

OBSERVING THE ORIGINAL STRUCTURE of the Sistine Chapel ceiling, which was divided into grids, Michelangelo had the idea of highlighting those existing divisions by painting pillars and other architectural dividers to give a three-dimensional feel to the ceiling. Place some dividers in one of your paintings and notice the difference they make.

Materials

✛ 2 pieces of 9-by-12-inch construction paper
✛ Ruler
✛ Pencil
✛ Paints (tempera, watercolor, acrylics, etc.)
✛ Scissors

1. Place one piece of paper horizontally on the table.

2. Lay your ruler horizontally across the top edge of the paper, and make a faint mark at the 4-inch point and again at the 8-inch point. Do the same at the bottom of the paper.

3. Trace some very light lines from the top marks to the bottom marks. This should divide your paper into three equal portions.

4. Draw a landscape scene over the whole sheet of paper. Include an object (a house, a tree, etc.), an animal, a person, or a group of these in each portion of your paper, over the landscape.

5. Erase the faint vertical lines.

6. Paint the picture, then put it aside to dry.

7. Place the second piece of paper horizontally on the table.

8. Draw two columns or trees, making sure they go from the bottom of the paper to the top.

9. Paint the columns or trees and let them dry, then cut them out.

10. Once your painting is dry, place the columns or trees on it, in the spots where you had the light lines.

11. Compare the painting with and without dividers. How do you think the dividers change the painting? Do they make the figures on your painting stand out more or less?

He complained of these difficult conditions in a long poem addressed to a friend, Giovanni da Pistoia:

I've already grown a goiter from this torture,
hunched up here like a cat in Lombardy
(or anywhere else where the stagnant water's poison).
My stomach's squashed under my chin, my beard's

pointing at heaven, my brain's crushed in a casket,
my breast twists like a harpy's. My brush,
above me all the time, dribbles paint
so my face makes a fine floor for droppings!

The poem continues to describe Michelangelo's painful position, bent backward "as a Syrian bow" and struggling to keep balance. What's

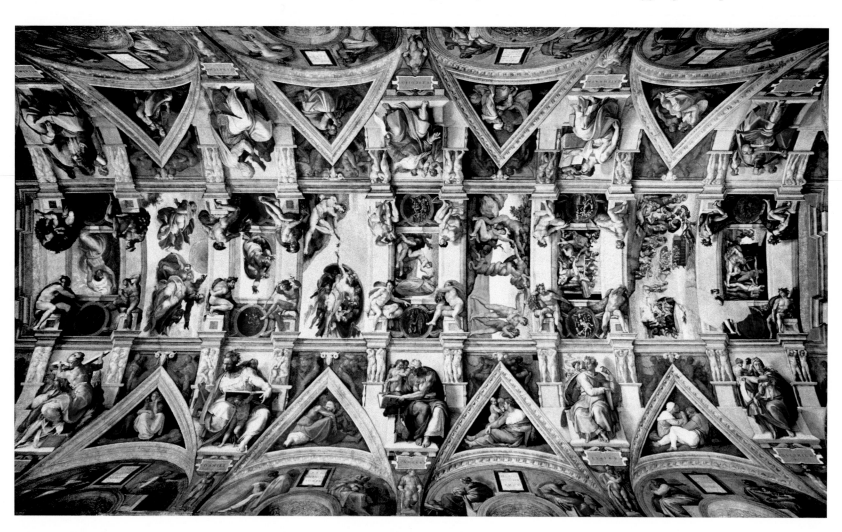

worse, the difficult posture and the consequent discomfort were affecting his thoughts. "Anyone shoots badly through a crooked blowpipe," he wrote, ending with a desperate appeal to his friend:

> *My painting is dead.*
> *Defend it for me, Giovanni, protect my honor.*
> *I am not in the right place—I am not a painter.*

Michelangelo had never considered himself a painter. His experience painting frescoes was limited to what he had learned 20 years earlier in Ghirlandaio's workshop. During the entire painting of the chapel, he continued to sign his letters, "Michelangelo, sculptor in Rome."

To achieve this astonishing project, he hired some assistants—as many as 13 in the course of four years—who carried water, cleaned brushes, mixed the colors, and painted the frames and, in the early stages, some of the figures. The first five came from Florence and were gathered mostly from Ghirlandaio's shop by Michelangelo's old friend Francesco Granacci, who also joined the work crew.

Immediately, Michelangelo faced several problems. For one thing, his team of helpers

✛ Map of the Sistine Chapel ceiling.

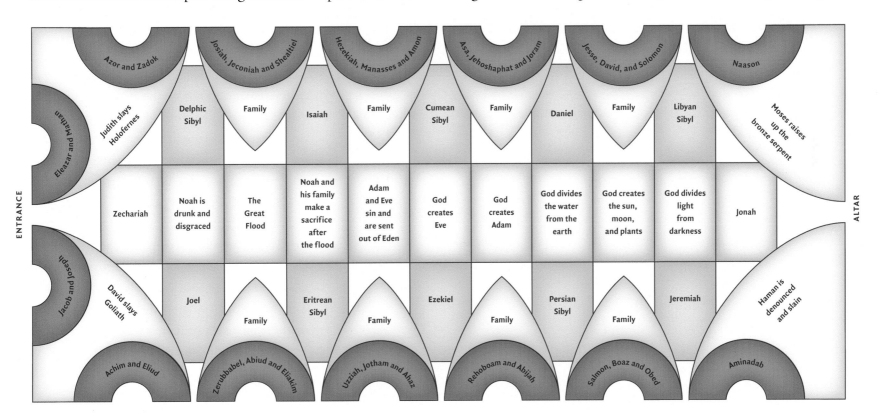

❧ Frescoes ❧

The Italian word *fresco* means "fresh" because it describes a method that requires paint to be applied to a wall while the **plaster** is still fresh. In this way, the painting becomes part of the wall.

Fresco painting is an ancient technique. Frescoes from ancient Egypt and Pompeii, Italy, are still around today. First, the artists or—more commonly—their assistants covered the wall with a coat of rough plaster. Over this, they applied a thinner plaster (*intonaco*) over an area they predicted they could finish plastering and painting in an eight-hour workday. This portion of plaster is called *giornata*, an Italian word that indicates the extension of the day. Changes in humidity and temperature, however, made these predictions difficult.

After applying the intonaco, the artists waited about two hours before painting. If, at the end of the day, the work was not finished, they had to work by candlelight before the plaster became too dry.

If the plaster was applied and set in different ways, the edges of each giornata would be visible. Normally, the assistant in charge of mixing the **pigments** had to make sure each day's colors matched those of the day before. Unfortunately, the final result could only be seen when the painting was dry. At that point, if a mistake was serious enough, the artist had to demolish the giornata and start again.

The design was usually drawn on a large paper called *cartone*. Then the outlines were carefully pricked, usually by an assistant, who would learn much by tracing the works of the master. Finally, the artist or an assistant would set the paper on the ceiling with nails and pass a bag of carbon dust over the lines. When the cartone was removed, the marks stayed on the wall. For large figures, the outline could be traced directly to the scene with a sharp tool (called a **stylus**). It was a complicated process and required the cooperation of many people.

was not used to the traditional building materials used by Romans, which dried more quickly than the ones used in Florence. That, combined with leaks in the chapel roof and an extremely cold winter, contributed to a very slow start. In addition, some mold on the walls caused some major flaws in the first fresco—so much that Michelangelo had to destroy much of it and start again.

What's more, since all his helpers came from Florence, they were forced to live together in Michelangelo's lodging, with frequent conflicts and complaints. Michelangelo liked to be in control, and the familiarity these people had developed with him in Ghirlandaio's shop didn't help their relationship at this time.

Besides, Michelangelo had to take care of other matters, such as the marble he had ordered for Julius's tomb, which was now either on its way or sitting at the port of Rome. He had to pay for the shipment from his own pocket and hope the pope would reimburse him.

His mind was also occupied by problems at home. By this time, Lodovico was working for Michelangelo, caring for the properties the artist had been buying, and purchasing new ones in his name. Michelangelo's brothers were also depending on the artist for support in their business ventures. Their frequent letters were full of grievances—mostly financial woes and family squabbles—which caused the artist much frustration.

"For twelve years now I have gone about all over Italy, leading a miserable life; I have borne every kind of humiliation, suffered every kind of hardship; worn myself to the bone with every kind of labour, risked my very life in a thousand dangers, solely to help my family," Michelangelo wrote to his brother Giovan Simone, who had become disrespectful toward their father. "If I do come home, I will give you cause to weep scalding tears."

In spite of this frequent exasperation, he cared for his family deeply. When Buonarroto became seriously sick, the artist, still deeply involved in the painting of the ceiling, was ready to jump on a stagecoach and hurry to his side, if necessary, "since men are worth more than money."

The Masterpiece

BY THE time Michelangelo started to work on the scene of Adam and Eve eating the forbidden fruit in the Garden of Eden, most of the technical problems were resolved, and the work was done more rapidly. At the end of this panel, Michelangelo felt confident enough to dismiss his Florentine workers and hire some local assistants.

Today, as visitors walk into the chapel, they see first the panel called *The Drunkenness of Noah* and move in reverse chronological order

CEILING PAINTER FOR A DAY

MOST OF THE TIME, Michelangelo painted standing up, as in the picture he drew next to the poem below. On a few occasions he probably knelt down. This activity can help you to understand some of the challenges of painting a ceiling in one of those positions.

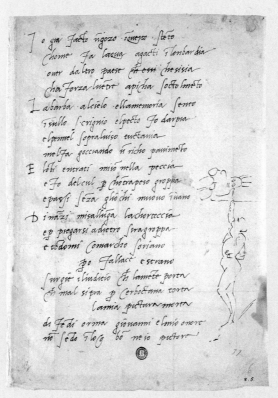

+ The original copy of Michelangelo's sonnet, with a self-portrait of the artist painting the ceiling frescoes in the Sistine Chapel.

Scala / Art Resource, NYv

Materials

+ Tape
+ A drawing you have already made or a page from a coloring book
+ Table or other platform you can kneel under
+ Crayons or markers

1. Using the tape, attach a drawing to the bottom of a tall table or perhaps a top bunk bed. You may find other suitable places in your house, but ask an adult to make sure you are safe.

2. Kneel under the table or on the bottom bunk, look up, and color your paper. How does it feel? Imagine doing this every day for many months.

This activity substitutes crayons and markers for paint in order to protect your eyes from drips, but Michelangelo used paint, which regularly dripped onto his face and into his hair and eyes.

of biblical events until standing under *The Creation of the Sun, Moon, and Plants.*

The best-known scene is *The Creation of Adam,* which depicts the hands of God and Adam about to touch—God active and Adam passive—in the first infusion of life. It is a very innovative scene. In earlier paintings, God was usually depicted as still and composed, while here Michelangelo conveys an energetic image of a powerful being hurtling through space.

Adam is represented as anatomically perfect and sincerely looking to God. His position seems perfectly natural but, as British Museum educators Kate Soden and Sarah Longair point out, it "in fact relies on an impossible dislocation of the upper body." This is a common habit with Michelangelo, who didn't hesitate to twist his figures in unnatural poses in order to better express their emotions.

It is often said that Michelangelo painted like a sculptor, because both his figures and the space around them give a feeling of three-dimensional perspective. To achieve this, Michelangelo started with a thin, almost transparent

✛ *The Creation of Adam* **is one of Michelangelo's most famous works.** Erich Lessing / Art Resource, NY

IN THIS ACTIVITY, you'll replicate how Michelangelo transferred his drawings to the ceiling, although he normally used charcoal instead of paint.

Materials

✦ 2 pieces of paper (any size)
✦ 1 sharp pencil
✦ Old towel or blanket
✦ Newspaper or a plastic sheet
✦ Tape
✦ Dark paint (any type)
✦ Large paintbrush
✦ Small paintbrush

1. Draw a simple picture on one piece of paper (or you can use something you have already drawn). If your papers are different sizes, draw on the smaller piece.

2. Fold the towel or blanket to obtain two or three layers, and put it on the table; then place your paper on top of the towel.

3. Using a sharp pencil, gently poke holes along the lines of your picture. Try to get the holes fairly close to each other without ripping the paper.

4. Remove the towel from under your paper.

5. Cover your table with newspaper or a plastic sheet to prevent spills.

6. Put the blank piece of paper on the covered table; then place the drawing on top. Keep both papers from moving by taping down the corners.

7. Use the large paintbrush to paint over the holes in the drawing with dark paint, making sure the paint is not too watery. If your picture looks very wet, wait until it dries.

8. Remove the top paper gently. You should see a trace of the drawing on the bottom paper.

9. Once the paint on the bottom paper is totally dry, use a small paintbrush to retrace the picture.

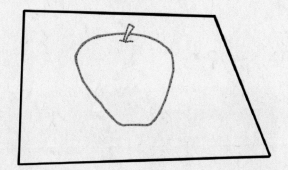

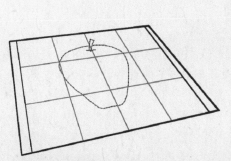

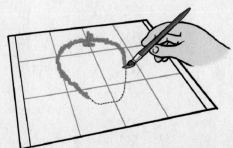

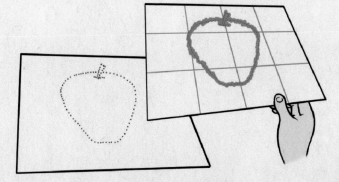

layer of color and built over it with small but dense brushstrokes, creating the equivalent of cross-hatching. To accentuate the perspective between figures, he sketched the ones in the distance quickly with the brush, without defining the details.

Since the painting was going to be about 68 feet above the observers' heads, he created some optical illusions. For example, in *The Creation of Adam*, he left the white of Adam's eye unpainted, so the gray plaster gives a sense of depth and mystery. To create shadows and depth in other areas of the ceiling, especially in the drapery, he placed different colors next to each other instead of darker shades of the same color.

The movements and positions of the bodies were also important. The prophet Jonah, for example, leans back to give the impression of a large space above him. Other prophets assume twisted positions to give a sense of restlessness, as if they were resisting the shape of the ceiling in an effort to come to life.

The ceiling was unveiled to the public on November 1, 1512. It immediately received wide acclaim. According to Condivi, "It brought him so much fame that it lifted him above all envy."

Michelangelo's brilliant colors have been gradually hidden under a thick coat of dirt produced by time, the use of smoky animal-fat candles in the chapel, and a misguided attempt by early restorers to protect the painting by adding a layer of glue, which only attracted more dirt. By 1980, when a new restoration was started, the painting was so dark it could hardly be seen. This restoration ended in 1994, returning most of the painting to its initial brightness.

This restoration encountered a certain amount of resistance, as some feared the harsh methods would strip the paintings of any finishing touches Michelangelo might have applied later. Most people today agree that the very visible and bright ceiling we have now is to be preferred to the previous obscured images.

✛ **The Prophet Jonah** in the Sistine Chapel frescoes (after restoration).

Trouble in Tuscany

WHILE MICHELANGELO worked busily in the narrow space under the Sistine's ceiling, momentous changes were taking place in his beloved Tuscany. In August 1512, Spanish troops financed by the pope and flanked by Cardinal Giovanni de' Medici (son of Lorenzo the Magnificent) marched toward Florence in an effort to regain the city for the Medici family. On the way, they stopped in Prato, about 15 miles from Florence, with the intention of sacking the city. The sack turned into a brutal massacre of more than 5,500 citizens, which provoked shudders of horror around Italy.

After the sack, when Giovanni and his brother Giuliano entered Florence as conquerors, the Florentines submitted out of fear, and the Medici returned to rule the city.

As on other occasions, his advice was to exercise prudence. "Be at peace," he wrote Buonarroto, "and don't make friends or be familiar with anyone, except God. Don't say anything good or bad to anyone, because one never knows how things will end. Mind your own things."

As for himself, he was quick to protect his name from any suspicion. "About the Medici, I never said anything against them except for what everyone else was generally saying, as in the case of Prato when even the stones, if they had a voice, would have spoken," he wrote his father.

ACTIVITY

SHADES OF COLOR

CREATE SHADES with a cross-hatching method of painting used by Michelangelo.

Materials
+ Pencil
+ Drawing paper
+ Large paintbrush
+ Tube of paint (tempera, watercolor, oil, or acrylic) of one color
+ Small paintbrush

1. Create a simple pencil drawing of a round object (a fruit, a ball, a vase, etc.).

2. Using the large paintbrush, color your drawing with a thin layer of paint.

3. With the small paintbrush and thicker paint, create small intersecting lines on your painting. Repeat a few times, especially on the side of the object that receives less light.

To ensure some level of safety, he appealed to one of his Medici friends, but continued to proceed with caution. "If [these measures] don't help," he told his father, "think about selling what we have, so we can go live somewhere else.... Take care of your life, and if you can't get as many honors as other citizens, be content with your bread and live well with Christ, in poverty, as I do here." As was typical of his letters, he concluded, "One must have patience and hope in God."

✠ FOR ✠
the LOVE
of FLORENCE

One must have patience.

—Michelangelo

A Mirror for All Italy

The Medici's influence and power increased greatly in 1513, when Pope Julius II died and was succeeded by Cardinal Giovanni de' Medici, who took the name of Leo X. Michelangelo and Leo were born in the same year and had studied together in the Medici's home.

At first, Leo didn't seem interested in employing Michelangelo. He preferred paintings to sculptures, favoring the young artist Raphael. In some ways, it was a good thing, because it gave Michelangelo time to work on Julius's tomb.

The same year, in fact, Julius's heirs signed a new contract with Michelangelo, granting him a steady income, an abundant supply of marble, and the free use

of a large house, with several stories, a reception room, a cellar, and two bedrooms. The property included a vegetable garden, a few wells, a stable, some smaller buildings for Michelangelo's servants and assistants, and a large yard where the artist grew figs, grapes, peaches, and pomegranates, and kept some chickens and a rooster.

The building stood on a busy street called Macel de' Corvi. The name (meaning "slaughterhouse of crows") refers to the numerous shops on the street, which sold not only crows but also other birds like thrush, pheasants, and capons. The house was better than the crowded studio where Michelangelo had lived before, and it was closer to the center of town, where the artist worked most of the time.

At the same time, Michelangelo had a feeling his circumstances would soon change. "I shall have to make a great effort here this summer to get my work done quickly," he wrote Buonarroto in June 1515, "as I expect soon to have to enter the pope's service."

His premonition came true. The same year, Leo, during a triumphal visit to Florence, envisioned a new **facade** for the church of San Lorenzo, where the Medici worshipped frequently. As a representative of that family, he thought a stately facade would communicate to the Florentines the Medici's role in the city's religious life. Michelangelo was considered for the job.

In spite of his inexperience in constructions, Michelangelo embraced the idea without any hesitation. Confident in his own instincts, he dismissed the help of an architect suggested by the pope and built a wooden model of the facade as he imagined it, including 12 classical columns in the style of the Roman Pantheon. He planned to make it out of pure white marble. Among the brownish buildings of Florence, this bright structure would have been a wonder.

He waited eagerly for the pope's approval. When he received it, he produced pages of drawings, specifying the needed measurements and shapes for every portion of the building, then traveled to Carrara and nearby Pietrasanta to find the purest marble.

He wanted each column to be carved out of a single block of stone. The probability of finding 12 perfect, enormous marble blocks was slim, and Michelangelo had to rely on a trusted helper to do much of the research. When a block was found, he inspected it in person. Over the years, he had learned to spot defects and to assess a block's strength by the sound of a few hammer blows.

On the other hand, he knew some flaws could still show up when the work was under way. To prevent unpleasant surprises, he quarried thicker blocks than needed so he could cut off the defected areas and still have enough to carve.

The quarries were about 90 miles from Florence. It took one day to reach the general location by horse and another day to climb the mountain by mule. The marble blocks were then laboriously transported back to Florence, a process that took about six months. At first, as usual, the workers moved each block to the valley floor by sleds, then to the seaside by oxcart. From there, since they couldn't send the stone straight to Florence by sea—as they would have done if it were going to Rome—they shipped it to Pisa by boat, then transported it by **barge** along the Arno River. Finally, they switched back to oxcarts around Signa, about eight miles west of Florence, where the river became too shallow for barges. The transportation depended much on the fullness of the river and the availability of oxen, which were in short supply during plowing season.

In the meantime, Michelangelo kept himself extremely busy. Besides traveling back and forth from Florence to the quarries (at least 19 times), he also went to Genoa to obtain adequate boats; bought or borrowed ropes, pulleys, and other instruments; commissioned especially long sleds; and supervised the opening and widening of a new road through the mountains, which was needed to move the marble from less utilized quarries.

It was a complex and expensive process. The extraction of the first column out of the mountain took four months of preparation and cost

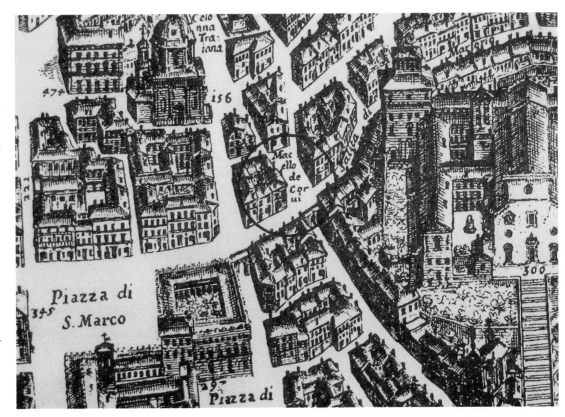

60 ducats, which was about double the yearly salary of a quarryman. The fee for transporting the marble to the city was also very high—often 10 times the price of the marble itself.

Each block weighed from 10 to 20 tons and could easily crush a person. In this case, the risk of injury was multiplied by 12 since there were 12 blocks. Once, Michelangelo wrote about a block of marble, "Someone got hurt while hauling it down. One man broke his neck and died immediately, and I was about to lose my life." Another time, a block of quarried marble

✚ **The location of Michelangelo's house, circled, on a 1676 map.** Alvaro de Alvariis

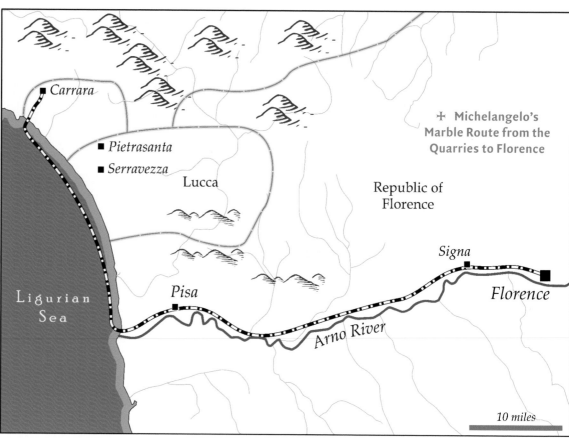

+ Michelangelo's
Marble Route from the
Quarries to Florence

10 miles

+ A reenactment of the ancient method
of transporting marble, called *lizzatura*. This
method was practiced until the 20th century,
when modern machines were adopted.
Elisabetta Paoletti Perini

fell into the river and "broke into a hundred
pieces.... All those who were around it, me included, had the narrowest escape from death."
He concluded with his frequent expression of
resignation, "One must have patience."

More Disappointments

IN 1519, just when the preliminary prepara-
tions were completed, Pope Leo canceled the
project. In the first two years of his papacy,
he had exploited all the riches Julius II had
accumulated. Besides, two young Medici
dukes, Lorenzo and Giuliano (respectively
the grandson and third son of Lorenzo the
Magnificent), had recently died, and a family
mausoleum seemed more necessary and af-
fordable than an imposing facade as a way to
inspire a greater appreciation for the Medici
in Florentines' hearts.

In a long and bitter letter (the second-longest he ever wrote), Michelangelo listed all his efforts and personal expenses, complaining of the insult he had received as a payment. The letter was to no avail, as the pope didn't change his mind. Thankfully, some of the marble could be used for the mausoleum.

Michelangelo found it difficult to be enthusiastic about this minor commission. The work proceeded slowly and came to an actual stop in 1522, after Leo's death, when the Dutch Adrian VI, an austere and frugal man, took his place.

Pope Adrian was not interested in art. In fact, he so disapproved of Europe's non-Christian past influencing art and theology that he wanted to destroy the Sistine Chapel ceiling, with its mythological and naked figures.

Michelangelo was alarmed. His anxiety, however, didn't last long. Adrian died in 1523, and Clement VII, another Medici and previous companion of the artist, became pope. "With regards to art, many things will be accomplished," Michelangelo wrote to his quarry supervisor.

A Busy Schedule

MICHELANGELO FIRST visited Pope Clement in December 1523. The visit went well. Clement was excited to use the artist's talents not only for the Medici Chapel but also for an impressive new project: a large library in honor of Lorenzo the Magnificent—the Laurentian Library—where the valuable collection of Medici books could be preserved.

Feeling appreciated, Michelangelo worked enthusiastically on both projects at once. The pope and the artist stayed in touch with friendly letters, writing up to three times per week. Clement asked many questions about the projects, getting into minute details, and flooded him with new ideas. On the other hand, he didn't try to control his protégé and often reminded him to work as he pleased.

Michelangelo's team of laborers and assistants worked hard on both the chapel and library, under the artist's close oversight. Wearing many hats at once, Michelangelo drew the plans, supervised the work, inspected the marble and other materials, recorded the workers' hours, and handed out their salaries.

To ensure the work was done according to his plans, he traced some architectural figures (for example, the bases of the columns) on paper **stencils** and transferred them to patterns of wood or tin that the marble carvers could copy.

Since paper was expensive, he often used the leftover scraps to keep track of his workers' names and the hours they worked, to record expenses, to count stone blocks, to sketch ideas, to draw and doodle, and to compose poems. His writing became smaller and smaller as he ran out of space.

✛ **Pope Clement VII.**

DRAW A RIDICULOUS GIANT

ONE OF CLEMENT'S MANY IDEAS was to build a giant statue in front of the church of San Lorenzo. For a while, Michelangelo dismissed the idea. When the pope insisted, writing as many as three more letters about the project, the artist pointed out his heavy workload and limited physical strength.

Michelangelo then made a new proposal. Switching to a humorous and sarcastic tone, he suggested that he could make a statue even larger than the pope had envisioned, and place it next to the barber's shop. On second thought, to keep the barber's entrance free, he proposed to set it on top of the shop. In winter, however, the barber would need to build a fire—the statue could hold a cornucopia, which would serve as a chimney. It could also have a hollow head to be used as a birdhouse for doves (a dovecote) or, even better, as a bell tower (a belfry), with the sound of bells coming out of its mouth. This was all in jest. In reply, the pope asked him to finish the mausoleum and the library, and never talked about the giant statue again.

Draw a giant according to Michelangelo's directions, and add your own details.

Materials

+ Paper
+ Pencil
+ Colored pencils, crayons, markers, or paints (optional)

1. Reread Michelangelo's description of the giant, at left.

2. Draw a picture of a barber shop.

3. Draw a giant on the shop's roof. You can follow Michelangelo's directions, including the belfry or dovecote, or come up with your own ideas for how to "improve" the statue. If you like, you can add color to accentuate the details.

4. Compare your drawing with friends' or classmates' pictures. Who came up with the silliest addition to their statues?

He often wrote poetry on the spot, surrounded by the noise of oxcarts coming and going, workers shouting orders, and the beating of hammers. Sometimes, he simply jotted down quick thoughts and truncated verses.

His papers reveal his patient and humorous relations with his pupils. While most workers at San Lorenzo were skilled professionals, there were also some apprentices who worked in exchange for art lessons. Some papers show skillful drawings next to incompetent copies—most likely Michelangelo's samples next to his pupils' renditions.

The papers were passed back and forth from teacher to student and were often filled with the type of amusing and monstrous drawings that were popular in the Renaissance. They also included Michelangelo's comments to his students: "Andrea [Italian name for Andrew], be patient," and "Draw, Antonio, draw, and don't waste time."

Around 1526, more than 100 workers were employed at San Lorenzo. Most of them came from Settignano and commuted daily by foot or on market carts. The overseers and the best marble carvers stayed in a house the artist had rented in Florence. As his biographer William Wallace tells us, nearly half of his crew had nicknames, including "the Stick, the Basket, the Little Liar, the Dolt, Oddball, Fats, Thorny, Knobby, Lefty, Stumpy, and Gloomy."

At times, the workers tested Michelangelo's patience, especially if he felt exploited or cheated. Most of the time, however, he had good relations with them and was ready to put up with their shortcomings.

"Topolino" ("Little Mouse"), for example, was a faithful and hardworking quarry supervisor from Carrara, who was convinced he had sufficient talent to be a sculptor. With every shipment of marble, he added a few small sculptures of his own, that invariably "made Michelangelo nearly die of laughter."

"You are a fool, Topolino, to want to make statues," Michelangelo said once, pointing out that a statue's lower legs were one-third of the proper size. Undeterred, Topolino extended the legs by adding a pair of boots, which caused Michelangelo to laugh even harder.

The crew labored six days a week from sunrise to sundown, taking care of the architectural blocks and ornaments. Usually, Michelangelo visited the work site around noon, stayed as long as necessary to oversee the project and give instructions, then went back to his workshop where he worked well into the night with one or two assistants, focusing on the statues. He spent a large amount of money on candles because he preferred those made of pure goat's tallow—a steadier source of light.

In this period, one of the busiest of his life, he usually slept with his clothes on and—following his father's advice—never bathed.

Only rarely, he gave himself a sponge bath. In fact, he kept his boots on his feet for so long that when he took them off some of his skin peeled off "like a snake's."

Sometimes overexertion got the best of him and he fell sick for a few days. His brother Buonarroto was especially concerned. "It seems to me," he wrote, "that you must value your person

63

more than a column, the whole quarry, the pope, and the whole world!"

Sunday, however, was a day of rest and church attendance for all. Michelangelo spent most Sundays with his family, where the faithful family servant, Mona Margherita, served festive and nourishing meals.

The Medici Chapel

THE MEDICI Chapel was intended as a burial chamber for the Medici family. As was typical of Michelangelo, however, he started to work on less important elements, reserving the tombs for the end.

He used this first encounter with architecture to study, imitate, and improve on the models of the masters who came before him. He was not afraid to create and surprise.

Outside, on top of the dome, Michelangelo placed a large **lantern** made out of the most expensive marble. In the Middle Ages, both the lantern and the number eight were symbols of the resurrection.

Inside, he aimed for an atmosphere of simplicity and somber quietness, accentuated by alternating gray stone (*pietra serena*) and white marble. The majority of the light comes from very high windows and a small hole in the dome (an imitation of the Pantheon dome), which softly fills the darkness below and lifts the visitor's gaze.

The walls include eight doors, but four are not real. Over each door stands a fake window, decorated by a single garland and supported by a bracket.

Today, the most prominent features of the chapel are the monuments to the young Medici dukes, standing on opposite walls. On one side is Giuliano, strong and confident, his casket topped by the allegorical figures of Night and Day. On the other side sits Lorenzo, pensive and melancholic, with Dusk and Dawn adorning his casket. Bent and twisted in restless and humanly unsustainable poses—in stark contrast with the stillness of the architecture—the four figures on the caskets represent the passing of time.

On a separate wall stands an unfinished statue of a Madonna with child, flanked by two saints that were carved later by other sculptors. The Madonna's mood fits the atmosphere around it. She looks melancholic, distant, and resigned, while her child vigorously turns around, apparently looking for her breast.

As usual, while following a traditional classical pattern Michelangelo breaks free from a close imitation of reality. For example, the two dukes' armor looks unrealistically skintight. Also, their features don't look at all like the young men looked in real life. Michelangelo refuted his critics by pointing out that a thousand years later no one would know how the young men had really looked. On the contrary, everyone would remember the idealized images the artist had depicted.

In 1527, a violent attack on the city of Rome by German and Spanish troops sent shock waves throughout Europe. Until then, Rome had been considered the unshakeable center of **Christendom**. After a series of massacres, raids, kidnappings, and other acts of violence, the raiders captured Pope Clement.

Taking advantage of the fall of the Medici pope, the people of Florence expelled the ruling family from the city and reinstated a free republic. Naturally, the work at the Medici Chapel and library came to a halt, and Michelangelo abandoned many statues before their completion. Some portions, however, seem to have been left unfinished by choice. For example, the legs of *Day* on Giuliano's monument are very detailed, so much so that we can see the bulging veins, while the face is completely blurred, as in the vision of someone who is just waking up.

While Michelangelo's unfinished works are often attributed to the necessity or desire to abandon his projects, in many cases (this one included) critics agree that the artist left some

✢ ABOVE: **The dome of the Medici Chapel, with the white marble lantern visible at lower right.** Jay8085, Flickr

✢ BELOW: **Interior of the Medici Chapel, with the tomb of Duke Giuliano de' Medici. Michelangelo worked on the tomb, off and on, for more than a decade.** Scala / Art Resource, NY

ONCE, MICHELANGELO ASKED one of his pupils to copy a drawing of a woman's head. The result was so poor that Michelangelo decided to cover it up by drawing a dress for the woman and blending the pupil's drawing with the woman's left sleeve.

Look at Michelangelo's drawing *Girl with a Spindle* at right. Can you see the head hidden in the folds of the sleeve?

Now it's your turn to hide a drawing inside another picture.

Materials
+ Paper
+ Pencil
+ Colored pencils, crayons, markers, or paints (optional)

1. Make a small drawing of anything you like.

2. Now hide your first picture by drawing another picture around it on the same paper and blending the two together (for example, blend your picture into the foliage of a tree, into the folds of a dress, or into the waves of the ocean). You can add color to further disguise your picture.

3. Show the finished picture to your friends and see if they can spot the hidden drawing.

+ A drawing in black chalk, named *Girl with a Spindle*, by Michelangelo and assistant, c. 1525. © The Trustees of the British Museum / Art Resource, NY

portions unfinished on purpose, as a poetic or artistic technique (equivalent to the **sfumato** technique used by Leonardo in his paintings).

The chapel was later completed by Michelangelo's followers Giorgio Vasari and Bartolommeo Ammannati, who remained very faithful to his plans. The chapel as it stands today is only a fraction of what Michelangelo had intended, but with its elegant and intriguing combination of impressive sculptures, fake columns, geometric shapes, and symbolic details, it remains one of his masterpieces.

The Laurentian Library

THE LAURENTIAN Library—the project Clement had envisioned for the collection of the Medici's books—stands only a few hundred feet from the chapel. The new structure was planned to stand on top of a **cloister**, in order to protect against possible floods. This location presented a challenge for Michelangelo, who had to ensure the older building was strong enough to hold a new construction, and had to engineer ways to bring the building materials to the top.

Today, visitors access the library through a majestic entrance hall, which includes, as in the chapel, fake windows and columns. The columns are positioned high up along the walls (rather than reaching from floor to ceiling like real columns), and are unrealistically held up

❖ Michelangelo's Diet ❖

One of Michelangelo's papers shows a list of food items, divided into three groups. Some think it was a shopping list, or three separate lists. Others believe it was a series of menus. Next to each entry, Michelangelo drew a picture of the corresponding item. Maybe the list was meant for a servant who could not read well. These are all suppositions. There is no way of knowing for sure what the list was for. In any case, the listed items were probably part of Michelangelo's diet.

The list is dated March 18, 1518, a time when Michelangelo was working at the quarries of Pietrasanta. It was Lent, a yearly period of 40 days when Roman Catholics traditionally ate a lighter diet (avoiding meats and rich foods) in remembrance of Jesus Christ's sufferings and crucifixion.

Here is Michelangelo's list:

Tortelli pasta, a herring, two bread rolls, and a jug of wine

Salad greens, four bread rolls, a plate of spinach, four anchovies, tortelli pasta, and wine (three different types)

Two bowls of fennel soup, a herring, six rolls, and wine

At other times of the year, Michelangelo enjoyed richer foods, including the renowned lard (cured pig fat) from Colonnata, near Carrara and Pietrasanta. Italians still enjoy this type of lard, especially thinly sliced on warm bread.

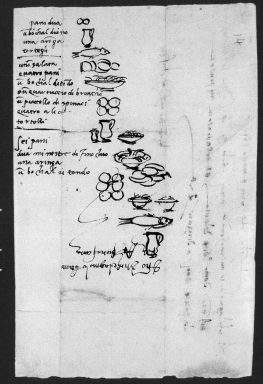

✝ Michelangelo's list of food items written on the back of a letter he received from a friend. Scala / Art Resource, NY

by a platform supported by small brackets, emphasizing the fantastic nature of these purely decorative elements.

The overall feeling of the place is one of silence and awe, accentuated by the imposing stairway—the main feature of the scene—which symbolically transports patrons from the noisy exterior to the quietness of the library.

In his plans, Michelangelo described the center stairs as a series of oval boxes, set one above the other and decreasing in size as they rise. The adjoining side stairs are rectangular and were meant for the servants who followed their mas-

ters. Along the way, there are two wider steps—one where the two side stairs join with the center portion, and the other at the top of the staircase. Both of these force the visitor to pause, making the experience of entering the library even more solemn and sobering.

The door at the top of the stairs is shaped like a window, with a frame all around, leading to a grandiose medieval-style library, where long rows of desks are divided by an aisle in the middle. The windows are arranged so that each one overlooks two desks. Each desk includes a seat, a reading stand, and a storage space underneath.

On the side of each desk is a list of the books that were once stored in that particular space. The books covered many subjects, such as theology, philosophy, astronomy, history, and literature. Readers were able to survey the lists, locate the book they wanted, and sit at the desk where the book was kept. If they needed to consult a different book, they had to change seats because the books were chained to the desk. The library is still open today to certain authorized users. The books, however, are not kept under the desks but in a separate area.

Construction of the library was completed in 1568 by Giorgio Vasari and Bartolommeo Ammannati. Architects still come from all over the world to admire this structure, which is considered by many the finest of all Renaissance libraries.

Wartime

EVENTUALLY, POPE Clement reconciled with the German emperor, and the Medici prepared to take back Florence. In spite of his previous ties with the Medici family and his current friendship with the Medici pope, Michelangelo sided with his native city.

In fact, he offered his skills as military engineer and was appointed director of the city's defense systems. Leaving military preparedness in the hands of an artist was not a new idea, as there was a common notion that artists could build anything, including fortifications. Leonardo da Vinci had drawn several plans for the defense of Milan. As usual, Michelangelo rose quickly to the task.

Defense had not changed much from ancient times, except for the invention of the cannon. To fend off cannonballs, the city walls had to be made thicker, lower, rounder, and slanted.

Michelangelo started with some geometric designs, often resembling fierce animals, such as crabs, lobsters with giant claws, or mythical insects and birds. He then placed these fortifications at crucial intersections on the city walls, to give them added strength and to create strategic **bastions**. For example, his crab-claw-shaped bastions allowed both a greater protection and a wider range of fire.

One of his greatest innovations was a star-shaped design, which was even used during the

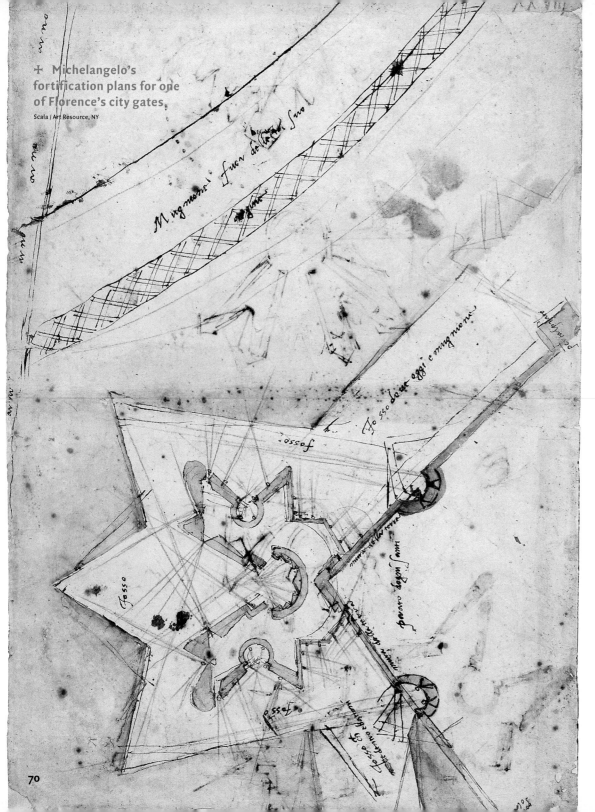

+ **Michelangelo's fortification plans for one of Florence's city gates.**
Scala / Art Resource, NY

American Civil War as an ingenious way of deflecting cannonballs. Due to the state of emergency, he didn't discount simple solutions, such as hanging mattresses outside the city walls to soften the blows of the enemy's artillery.

The Pain of Death and Defeat

IN 1528, Florence's problems were compounded by a sudden epidemic of the **plague**. To save himself and his family, Buonarroto closed his shop in Florence and retired with his loved ones to Settignano. In spite of this precaution, he fell ill and died.

It was a time of great sorrow for Michelangelo, who loved his brother deeply. After paying for the funeral and returning the **dowry** to Buonarroto's wife, he committed himself to the care of their children: Francesca, who was not yet nine; Lionardo, six years old; and Simone, who was barely two. At that time, if a man died, his father's family had sole custody of the children.

Michelangelo entrusted Francesca to the care of a convent, where she would be raised until she was of marriageable age. He paid for her tuition and bought her some fine clothes. Lionardo and Simone moved in with their 84-year-old grandfather in Settignano. Soon, however, Lodovico realized Lionardo was more than he could handle, and Michelangelo took the boy into his house in Florence.

BUILD A DOUBLE-STAR FORTIFICATION

MICHELANGELO DESIGNED very original and inventive fortifications. You can start with a simple double-star fortification and work your way to something more ambitious.

Materials

✛ 9-by-11-inch piece of construction paper (or larger)
✛ Pencil
✛ Ruler
✛ Scissors
✛ Glue

1. Measure and cut three strips of construction paper, 2 inches high and 11 inches long, and lay them lengthwise on a table or other flat surface.

2. Make 1-inch marks along the top and bottom edges of one of your strips.

3. Starting from the left, fold the paper along the first mark, and press to form a crease.

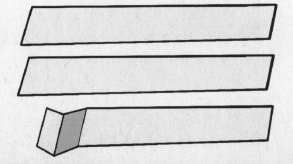

4. Flip the paper over and crease on the second mark.

5. Continue to fold accordion-style, creasing at each mark, until you reach the last mark. You will have one extra inch of paper.

6. Unfold the paper and shape it into a star, joining the ends of the paper.

7. Glue the extra inch of paper to the opposite side to close the star.

8. Make two-inch marks along the top and bottom edges of the other two strips.

9. Fold the strips accordion-style. You will have one extra inch of paper for each strip.

10. Glue the extra inches of one piece strip to the ends of the other strip, then open in the shape of a star.

11. Set the small star inside the large star. These will be the double walls for your city.

If you want to try different shapes, you can look for Michelangelo's plans online, or design your own.

Michelangelo bought little "Nardo" some tailor-made clothes, a pair of clogs, a furry black hat, a Latin grammar book for beginners, and some useful everyday items, including a silver spoon and a pocket knife with scissors.

Sadly, after seven months, he had to send the boy back to Lodovico. The republic of Florence, still in a state of emergency, requested that the artist travel to other cities to inspect their fortifications.

One of these cities was Ferrara, northeast of Florence, where Duke Alfonso d'Este owned some of the best fortifications in Europe and a large arsenal of cannons. On this occasion, the duke offered Florence his advice, and possibly his support, in exchange for a painting by Michelangelo. The artist complied, choosing a mythological subject that was in line with Alfonso's taste. In the long run, however, Alfonso decided not to help Florence, and the painting was sold in France by one of Michelangelo's assistants.

In the meantime, many affluent people were moving out of Florence. Lodovico and the boys moved to a village near Pisa, where, unfortunately, little Simone died from unknown causes. Gismondo described the family's pain as that of "a knife piercing the heart."

Even Michelangelo wavered in his loyalty to his city. In September, maybe as a result of a threat, he left for Venice with two companions and entertained some thoughts of moving to France.

The Florentine government, however, declared him a rebel. The punishment for rebels was confiscation of goods. To avoid casting himself and his family into sudden poverty, humiliation, and possibly exile, Michelangelo returned to Florence in November, just as the city was besieged by Medici troops.

While Michelangelo's fortifications proved highly successful in keeping the enemies out, on August 10, 1530, after a 10-month siege, Florence was forced to surrender because of starvation, exhaustion, and treason. It was a most dangerous time for Michelangelo, who had been deeply involved in the republican struggle. While the Medici reclaimed power, he hid with friends to avoid capture.

Clement granted the artist forgiveness and restored his salary so he could resume work at San Lorenzo. By this time, however, Michelangelo was "urged on more by fear than by love." Furthermore, his family needed the financial support, since the enemy forces had pillaged the countryside and food was scarce for people who, like the Buonarroti, depended largely on agricultural profits.

In 1531, Lodovico died and Michelangelo became officially responsible for the family's well-being. It was a role he had informally held for years, sometimes with annoyance but always with a strong feeling of duty. Lodovico's death followed shortly after Buonarroto's. Michelangelo described the intensity of his double sorrow and the depth of his love and devotion by using images he knew best:

Painted like life my brother stands to me,
Thou [Father] art a sculptured image in my heart.

The artist found comfort as he thought of his father in Heaven:

There is no cloud to dim your shining light,
No chance nor need to bind your onward way,
No time to urge you with its rapid flight.

For some time, Michelangelo had felt the effects of aging in his own body, and building tombs had encouraged his meditations on death and the afterlife. He was 56—an age that was considered old at that time of frequent wars, plagues, and limited medical knowledge—and most of his contemporaries were reaching the ends of their lives.

The following year, Alessandro de' Medici, a rough and despotic man, took control of Florence and asked Michelangelo to design a new

✛ A reconstruction of a 16th-century cannon belonging to Duke Alfonso d'Este.
Ed Kilar

fortress. Strengthening a dictator's military powers was the last thing Michelangelo wanted to do. Longing to leave that uncomfortable situation, he made several trips to Rome, where other Florentine republicans had fled.

Finally, in September 1534, after hearing that Clement, his only Medici friend and protector, was on the verge of dying, the artist escaped Florence without much preparation, never to return.

JUDGMENT
✠ and GRACE ✠

The power to change fate is God's alone.

—MICHELANGELO, SONNET 274

The Last Judgment

Rome recovered slowly from the devastation of the 1527 sack. Buildings were being rebuilt and repaired, appreciation for the great city was renewed, and fresh ideas found fertile ground. By the time he escaped Alessandro de' Medici's dictatorial rule, Michelangelo had a number of close friends in the ancient city, especially within the community of exiled Florentines.

One of these friends had kept the house at Macel de' Corvi running well over the years, tending to the garden and the animals—including the cats, who had been "greatly lamenting" the artist's absence, even if they were "not lacking food." When Michelangelo arrived, it was time to harvest peaches and pomegranates.

Less than a month after Clement's death, the body of cardinals elected a new pope, who took the name of Paul III. Paul III was only seven years older than Michelangelo. A lover of the arts, he was eager to employ the artist's talents.

Pope Clement had already helped Michelangelo negotiate a compromise with Julius's heirs for the completion of the tomb. He had also discussed the idea of painting a scene of the Last Judgment on the end wall of the Sistine Chapel. Paul III went further on both accounts. The artist was to paint the whole end wall of the chapel, and the work on Julius's tomb was to be suspended.

"For thirty years I have had this wish [of hiring you]," Paul explained, "and now that I am pope, can I not gratify it?"

Free from other obligations, Michelangelo, who had not painted a fresco for more than 20 years, embraced the new project with excitement. He started to prepare large drawings and to oversee the preparation of the wall, which included the destruction of previous frescoes. Before laying the plaster, he asked that the two windows by the altar be blocked by bricks. He also required the construction of an inner brick wall in order to avoid a buildup of dust.

The pope inspected the progress regularly and with great interest. He even took an escort of at least 10 cardinals to visit Michelangelo at his home on its lowly market street. There, he examined the sketches and most likely discussed the **theological** meaning of the scenes.

Over time, the two developed a close friendship, and the artist was always ready to share with the pope the frequent gifts his nephew Lionardo sent him from Florence—some bottles of Trebbiano wine, fresh sheep's milk cheese, and fruit.

It must have been odd for Michelangelo to start a new masterpiece underneath the work he had done 20 years earlier. The new subject was a logical conclusion of the first. On the ceiling, he had painted the biblical accounts of the creation of man and of some of the earliest scenes of biblical history. On this wall, he was to show the Bible's vision of the world's end with the Second Coming of Jesus and the Last Judgment of all mankind.

The Last Judgment had been a frequent scene in medieval art—normally organized in an orderly and predictable manner, with a static Christ in the middle, the "saved" on his right, and the "damned" on his left. While preserving this basic composition, Michelangelo brought energy and originality to the traditionally passive scene by depicting a younger, stronger, more commanding Christ figure and more intensely involved apostles and saints, while the saved rise toward heaven and the damned sink or are pulled frighteningly down to hell.

The predominant color of the background is an intense shade of blue. Encouraged by the pope, Michelangelo didn't spare any expense and for the background used what is considered the most costly pigment in history—crushed **lapis lazuli** stone.

Most of the time, he had only one helper, nicknamed Urbino because he was born in a **duchy** by the same name, in a town about 100 miles east of Florence. Usually, Urbino ground and mixed the pigments, prepared the plaster, and painted a few minor figures. *The Last Judgment* was completed in almost six years but is so unified that it looks as if it had been done in one day. It was unveiled on October 31, 1541, on the eve of All Saints' Day, a Roman Catholic festival.

Immediately, it provoked both admiration and criticism. While Michelangelo might have thought it appropriate that the dead should rise without their clothes, some people objected to a mass of naked bodies covering the altar wall. There were also some theological concerns with Michelangelo's unconventional ideas.

For example, the saints, deprived of their halos, are almost indistinguishable from the damned. The angels are equally stripped of their wings, and Christ of his traditional beard. Mary, crouched down behind Christ with her hands close to her face, appears as a humble spectator instead of the **mediator** many had

✝ **Michelangelo's *The Last Judgment*.**
The Art Archive at Art Resource, NY

come to trust. What was the point of introducing so many unfamiliar images?

These concerns were particularly alarming at that time, as theologians on the other side of the Alps were boldly contesting many foundational tenets the Roman Catholic Church had developed over the centuries.

Ultimately, however, the church addressed only the problem of nudity, which Pope Pius IV ordered to be covered in 1564. The job was given to Daniele da Volterra, a friend and pupil of Michelangelo. In spite of being a talented artist on his own merits, Daniele went down in history as a *braghettone*, which can be loosely translated as "pants maker."

Family and Friends

IN SPITE of all his work, Michelangelo still kept up-to-date with his family's news. He must have been overjoyed when his niece Francesca married Michele Guicciardini, a nobleman from a prominent family, and again when she had a baby boy. The Buonarroti family was continuing. His next hope was that his nephew Lionardo would find a good wife and have a son to carry on the family name.

✝ Saint Bartholomew is shown in this detail of *The Last Judgment* on the wall of the Sistine Chapel. He holds his own skin in one hand. Some believe this skin is a distorted self-portrait of Michelangelo. Scala / Art Resource, NY

THE ARTIST AND THE ASSISTANTS

ASSISTANTS LIKE URBINO prepared pigments, materials, and surfaces and painted some portions of the picture, such as the background and some minor figures. Work with one or two friends. One can be the artist and the others can be the assistants.

Materials
✛ Paper or poster board
✛ Pencil
✛ Paints

1. The artist draws a sketch of the picture he or she wants to paint. It might help to use a large piece of paper or poster board so that the artist and assistants have room to work together.

2. Look at the picture and decide which portions the assistants will draw and paint (probably the background and some minor figures).

3. The assistants draw their portions of the picture.

4. The artist fills in any missing details and corrects the assistants' work if needed.

5. Now everyone can work together to paint the picture, with each person painting the sections that he or she drew.

You can try this activity again to give someone else a turn to be the main artist.

On the other hand, his busy schedule limited his correspondence with his family so much that, at one point, Francesca was afraid he had forgotten her. Even his letters to Lionardo were short and to the point, and he refused a visit Lionardo and Michele had planned to make him. "I am so busy I don't have time to take care of you, and every small thing is a huge bother, including writing this," he replied. "Cooking for you is the last thing I need!"

Some believe Michelangelo's legendary impatience was exacerbated by aging. In his 60s, he didn't have the same strength and stamina he had displayed in the past. Mounting the scaffold and maintaining uncomfortable po-

❧ Nudity in Renaissance Art ❧

Renaissance artists found inspiration in ancient Greek and Roman works and adopted the classical idea of the male nude as symbol of glory, health, beauty, and geometric harmony. In ancient Greece, athletes competed in the nude, so it was natural for Greeks to associate the naked male body with triumph and strength. Female nudes were rare and were usually limited to goddesses of fertility and procreation.

The portrayal of naked bodies was not usually sexual, but because some mythological stories include suggestive material, their depictions do too.

After the fall of the Roman Empire and the rise of Christendom, nudity in art became scarce, with the exception of some religious scenes, such as the creation of Adam and Eve and the Last Judgment. Typically, saints in heaven were portrayed with clothes and people in hell were naked.

The classical nude came back as a frequent artistic theme and respectable art form after the 13th century. Women, however, were rarely used as models. One main reason for this was convenience: workshops were filled with men, and it was easy for an artist to ask a boy apprentice to model a pose, and then later modify the features and add female clothing. The use of male models is visible in some of Michelangelo's pictures, such as the sibyls in the Sistine Chapel, which look particularly masculine. On the other hand, Michelangelo also created some very delicate female images, both in painting and in sculpture.

At that time, few women became artists because they weren't given the opportunity to do so. Training under male teachers, especially in workshops where male nudes were studied, was out of the question. The few women who became artists were trained by their fathers or close family members.

In 1563, the Roman Catholic Council of Trent insisted that "figures shall not be painted or adorned with a beauty exciting to lust." Being quite generic, these guidelines were interpreted by church leaders as they saw fit.

sitions for hours was becoming more taxing. Shortly before completing *The Last Judgment*, he fell from the scaffold and injured his leg. Still, he resumed working as soon as he could get out of bed. His only day of rest was Sunday, when the chapel was used for worship. Then he attended church, caught up with his correspondence, and visited friends.

One of his closest friends in Rome was a young man named Tommaso de' Cavalieri, a nobleman who, for a time, received some drawing lessons from the artist. The two met in 1532, when Michelangelo was still in Florence, and they remained friends until the artist's death. From time to time, Michelangelo sent Tommaso some drawings, which the young man proudly shared with the nobles, bishops, and cardinals of Rome, provoking their jealousy. Today we would say they went viral, because they were reproduced in many media, including carvings.

He also wrote poems for Tommaso. The passionate tone of these rhymes and the sensual content of some drawings (illustrations from Greek mythology) have led some to believe his feelings for the young man were more than a fatherly love for a young pupil. It is hard to judge events so distant in the past, especially since similar expressions of love and depictions of mythological stories were at that time fairly common and are present in other poems by Michelangelo.

Some rumors, however, must have spread even in his day, because Michelangelo devoted at least two poems to defending the chastity of his feelings for Tommaso against those "who always see themselves in others."

In 1545, Tommaso married a Roman noblewoman and had two children, Mario and Emilio (who became a famous composer).

At home, Michelangelo's best friend was his assistant Urbino, who had been working with him since the early 1530s and shared Michelangelo's home at Macel de' Corvi, together with Urbino's wife and children. The artist's love for Urbino provoked the jealousy of Lionardo and other relatives. Michelangelo had never shown so much affection and favoritism to any other assistant and had never paid such a high salary. Besides, Urbino gave the impression of being overly protective of his mentor, keeping some suitors at a distance and making sure most of Michelangelo's servants came from his own family.

These complaints didn't bother Michelangelo, who was growing increasingly disinterested in the practical affairs of his house and trusted Urbino almost blindly, not only with his finances but also to deliver important, sensitive, and even dangerous messages.

In fact, his political and religious allegiances were forcing him to watch over his correspondence more carefully than ever. Politically, he shared the exiles' dream of freeing Florence

from the Medici's tyranny, particularly after 1537, when Alessandro was assassinated and, after a short-lived republican resistance, another Medici, Cosimo I, established an even more dictatorial rule.

The clearest expression of Michelangelo's desire for a free republic was a small statue he sculpted in 1538 for a like-minded friend: an image of Marcus Brutus, the Roman senator who had taken part in the murder of Julius Caesar. While traditionally Brutus had been considered a villain, in recent times he had been seen as a symbol of the struggle against tyrants. This symbol was especially clear at that time, as Alessandro, like Caesar, had been killed by a relative.

Another controversial group of Michelangelo's friends was engaged in a different struggle—an effort to reform what they believed to be an immoral church.

The church's corruption and abuses had been long-standing subjects of ridicule in popular jokes and humorous books. Most people, however, had come to accept them as inevitable rotten spots on a still fairly edible apple. When protesting voices became too uncomfortable (as in Savonarola's case), they were eventually crushed. Overall, the church leaders tolerated the protests as passively as most people had come to tolerate the abuses.

Everything changed when a German monk, Martin Luther, attacked not only the church's corruption but its basic theology. In his view, God's favor cannot be earned or merited but is a gift that is received simply by believing the **gospel**. The Roman Catholic Church condemned this teaching and punished those who followed it. Michelangelo, who had been concerned about his own spiritual state at least since the days of Savonarola, became very interested in this renewed emphasis on faith alone.

In Italy, Martin Luther's message was promoted by a group of believers known as the Spirituali. One of the leaders of this movement was the noblewoman and renowned poet Vittoria Colonna, who had become a widow at a very young age. Michelangelo met her around 1537, when he was 62 and she was 45. Immediately, he was impressed by the depth of her wisdom and biblical understanding. The two shared many letters and poems about personal feelings, art, and religion. As with Cavalieri, Michelangelo's poems are expressions of fervent love and admiration. In this case, however, they also communicate his spiritual dependence on Vittoria, whom he called "the soul and the heart of my fragile life."

Michelangelo made several drawings and paintings for Colonna, often on religious themes—especially Jesus's crucifixion or removal from the cross. In these works, Jesus was no longer the composed man depicted in most medieval paintings. He agonized on the cross or drooped listless in the arms of his mother or supported by angels. In one of these pictures, Michelangelo added some words from Dante's *Divine Comedy*: "They devote no thought to how much blood it costs." This emphasis on Jesus's sacrifice and the blood he shed on the cross to reconcile sinners to God was a common theme for the Spirituali.

❧ Sonnets and Madrigals ❧

Michelangelo mostly wrote two types of poems: sonnets and madrigals. *Sonnet* comes from an Italian word meaning "little sound." Italian sonnets are composed of two parts. The first part (called an octave) includes eight lines, with the first line rhyming with the fourth, fifth, and eighth. The second, third, sixth, and seventh lines rhyme with each other. An octave's rhyme scheme is normally shown by the pattern ABBA ABBA. The second portion (called a sestet) is composed of six lines that can rhyme in different ways: CDECDE or CDCDCD.

Madrigals are musical compositions, usually sung by several voices without the accompaniment of musical instruments. Some of Michelangelo's madrigals were set to music during his lifetime. His grandnephew Michelangelo Buonarroti the Younger wrote many madrigals.

The Pauline Chapel

MICHELANGELO HAD barely finished *The Last Judgment* when Pope Paul III asked him to paint two frescoes in a chapel behind St. Peter's—the Pauline Chapel, which was connected to the papal palace.

The pope had already employed other architects and artists to build and decorate the chapel, and now that Michelangelo was available, he wanted to include some of his art. Specifically, he asked him to paint the scenes of the Conversion of Saint Paul on the left wall and the Crucifixion of Saint Peter of the right wall.

Michelangelo had not yet finished the tomb of Julius II, and the pope's heirs were constantly reminding him of the unfulfilled commission. When the artist raised this objection, Paul III sent a message to the heirs, who were forced to come to a compromise. They made a final contract with Michelangelo, requiring him to sculpt only three figures and leave three more to a trusted helper. Michelangelo worked simultaneously on the tomb and the chapel.

The two frescoes in the Pauline Chapel took almost eight years from start to finish, even if they were much smaller than *The Last Judgment*, which he had finished in six years. Michelangelo was getting old and felt even older. Twice he had to interrupt the work because of a serious illness. Besides, he was working at the same time on the tomb for Julius II and insisted on employing his friend Urbino almost exclusively. His eyesight was also starting to fail, so much so that Vittoria Colonna ordered him a custom-made pair of glasses from Venice—the major center of glass production.

Traditionally, paintings of Saint Paul's conversion showed the moment when he was called by Christ to turn from an eager persecutor of Christians into an apostle of the gospel to many nations. While keeping faithful to the scene, Michelangelo broke with tradition in many ways.

First, unlike other similar portrayals, Michelangelo made Christ, and not Paul, the protagonist of the scene. Paul lies helpless on the ground, overtaken by fright, literally blinded by the flash of light, and barely able to lift his arm to Christ in a plea for mercy. Some believe Michelangelo identified himself

ACTIVITY · BE A RENAISSANCE POET

MICHELANGELO AND HIS FRIENDS wrote short poems to each other as a fun and witty way of communicating their ideas and feelings. To a friend whose poem praised his statue *Night* in the Medici Chapel, Michelangelo, embittered by his city's loss of freedom, adopted the voice of Night to reply:

Dear to me is sleep and better to be stone (A)
So long as shame and sorrow still prevail. (B)
Not to see, not to feel is great avail. (B)
Hence, do not wake me, speak in a quiet
*   tone. (A)*

Try writing a short poem using Michelangelo's most common rhyme scheme (ABBA). For example, you could say:

I want to sing a song of days gone by, (A)
enchanted castles and dragons breathing
*   flames, (B)*
unselfish knights and courageous dames. (B)
Let's just go there together, you and I. (A)

Materials
✦ Paper
✦ Pen or pencil

1. Look at the samples provided above, or look for other examples of Michelangelo's sonnets here: http://publicdomainreview.org /collections/the-sonnets-of-michelangelo -1904-edition/.

2. Write your own short poem, keeping the same pattern of rhymes, with the first line rhyming with the fourth, and the other two rhyming with each other (ABBA).

with Paul as he was also undergoing a spiritual conversion. In fact, while most accounts place Paul's conversion in his youth, Michelangelo portrays him as an old man, closer to his own age.

Second, Christ's appearance and posture differ from traditional medieval portrayals. In this picture, Christ is not descending from heaven in the customary composure and imperturbable majesty. Instead, he invades the scene head-first, extending his powerful arm within the flash of light, in the direction of Paul's feeble hand. This portrayal raised some objections. One of Michelangelo's contemporaries remarked that Christ, "without any seriousness and any decorum, seems to plummet from the sky in a scarcely honorable act."

Another innovation is the use of color and light. Unlike previous paintings of Saint Paul's conversion, this one is mostly composed of vivid hues of red, yellow, and green, emphasizing the contrast of light and darkness. The viewer's eye is immediately caught by Christ's red robe, while Paul's red coat—not as bright—helps to make a visual connection between the apostle and his Lord.

The mass of people in the scene also differs from previous portrayals of this event, in which the masses were normally passive. Here, Christ's descent causes an absolute upheaval. The crowd, disordered and confused, flees in all directions. Paul's horse also runs away in

✛ In *The Conversion of Saint Paul*, Michelangelo depicts a more commanding, less passive Christ figure (reaching down in the upper left) than was traditionally painted or sculpted. Scala / Art Resource, NY

fear while a man tries to help Paul get back on his feet.

Finally, unlike any previous painting depicting the same event, Michelangelo's includes a crowd in heaven—made up of both saints and

angels, who are watching the scene with an equally strong display of emotions. In the original painting, the distinction between the saints and angels was clear because only the angels were naked. As with other works by Michelangelo, this fresco was edited by later popes.

The second fresco in the chapel depicts the death of Saint Peter, who, according to tradition, asked to be crucified upside down because he didn't feel worthy to die in the same manner that Jesus had. Being a more sober subject, *The Crucifixion of Saint Peter* was painted on the wall less exposed to the light.

Originally, Paul III wanted Michelangelo to paint an image of Jesus giving Peter the symbolic keys of the church. It seemed like a fitting choice at a time when Protestants were challenging the pope's supremacy. Michelangelo, however, had a different idea.

Once again he made some unexpected choices. As a subject, he chose Peter's crucifixion. Unlike most previous artists, he depicted the moment before the actual crucifixion, as the cross is being raised head-down (according to the traditional account).

To many, this is one of Michelangelo's most powerful paintings. Peter, the central figure, twists his head and shoulders, seeming to struggle to face the spectator. The size of his body, disproportionally large, emphasizes its centrality. Around Peter, the crowd watches and participates with expressions of horror, fear, sorrow, pity, or cruelty. Any visitor to the chapel will immediately feel Peter's piercing, angry glance, which seems to follow the onlooker. This total involvement of the viewer is typical of modern—rather than medieval—art.

Since cardinals met to choose new popes in the Pauline Chapel, and the Roman Catholic Church claimed Peter as the first pope, Peter's stern look has been traditionally interpreted as a grave reminder to the rich and powerful cardinals of the essence of true Christianity.

This idea seems supported by the fact that Peter's hair is cut in the fashion that was typical of monks. This type of haircut (called tonsure) was a medieval tradition, not in use in Peter's day, and was a symbol of purity and contempt for earthly goods.

Two people in this fresco bear a resemblance with Michelangelo: an old man on the lower right and another man with the characteristic turban sculptors wore to protect their heads from marble dust. Many see in these two images an attempt by Michelangelo to "sign" his work and identify with the participants.

The two paintings were completed in 1549. Michelangelo had planned to continue to paint the rest of the chapel, but the project was interrupted by the death of Paul III.

✠ AT ✠
the SERVICE *of*
a TROUBLED
CHURCH

I serve for the love of God, in whom is all my hope.

—MICHELANGELO, TO HIS NEPHEW LIONARDO

The "Tragedy" of Julius's Tomb

Michelangelo worked on the tomb for Julius II while he was painting the Pauline Chapel. The terms of the final contract, negotiated by Paul III, could be met fairly easily. The artist was supposed to deliver only three statues, and he had three that were already almost completed, depicting Moses and two slaves. Instead of using these, however, he changed his mind. In place of the slaves, he decided to sculpt two women who represented the Contemplative Life and the Active

✠ The tomb of Pope Julius II in the church of San Pietro in Vincoli. © Vanni Archive / Art Resource, NY

Life (later identified with Rachel and Leah, wives of Israel's patriarch Jacob).

There could be many reasons for this change. Michelangelo had sculpted the slaves in his youth, when he focused on recapturing the beauty of classical art—which often depicted the male body—and exploring a wide range of movements as means of expression. By this time, however, his mind was absorbed by spiritual thoughts, which could be better represented by these women: Rachel, visibly overtaken by spiritual yearnings, and Leah, calmly working out her faith in this world.

Besides, in the new, downscaled structure, Moses had become the focal point and the women's smaller size and restricted movements provided a better balance to his imposing and fearsome features—his muscular, tense body; his turbulent hair and beard; his fierce gaze; and his horns (symbolizing the beams of light that, in the biblical account, emanated from his face when he descended from Mount Sinai).

In any case, these two statues represent a deliberate choice and took much of the artist's time and strength. The result is one of the finest examples of female beauty in Michelangelo's art.

Michelangelo probably reworked the statues over time, since the description he gave to Condivi conflicts with the finished work. For example, he said Moses's left hand was holding his chin, but it actually rests on his lap, catching the ends of his beard. He also said the Active Life holds a mirror with one hand and a garland of flowers with the other, but the two objects she holds look more like a torch and laurel crown.

According to recent researchers, headed by Antonio Forcellino, sometime after March 1542 Michelangelo literally turned Moses's head and torso to one side. In order to do this, he had to sculpt a new nose where the chin was and had to shift one leg. In the process, one knee became a little smaller than the other, and Michelangelo had to mask the difference by covering it with a drape.

Why did the artist go to so much effort to change a statue that was virtually finished? Some think he wanted to impart a feeling of greater motion. Michelangelo didn't give a plausible explanation. Instead, he justified the change with his typical Tuscan humor: "You know," he told Vasari, "the Moses heard us speaking the other day and, in order to understand us better, turned his head."

Vasari noted that on the tip of Moses's nose there was a piece of the marble that once belonged to his cheek. The story was viewed with skepticism until recent works of restoration proved it was true.

As for the changes in *Leah*, Michelangelo might have simply changed his mind. Forcellino, however, has suggested Michelangelo might have changed only the statue's description, to avoid—in a controversial religious climate—any words that recalled the language used in the Spirituali's most popular writing, *The Benefit of Christ's Death* (where good works are described as a light).

Within this new, resized mausoleum, the statue of Pope Julius takes a place of lesser importance. Tucked in an upper niche, he looks small, submissive, and pensive—very different than the popular image of the warrior pope. Instead of standing with his arm raised or holding a symbol of his position, as in most portrayals of popes, Julius is reclined, his head bowed, resting his empty hands under his chest, as if reflecting on the vanity of this life.

Since Michelangelo was required to finish only three statues, for years the one of Julius has been attributed to another sculptor. Recent works of restoration, however, have allowed for closer examination, raising some evidence that Michelangelo might have played a large part in designing and sculpting this statue. Besides, the overall depiction of the pope as a humble shepherd of souls would be consistent with the artist's nonconformity and religious convictions.

The other statues—a sibyl, a prophet, and a Madonna with child—are almost exclusively the product of other hands.

The tomb's difficult history of delays, threats, disappointments, and frustrations prompted Condivi to call it a "tragedy." In spite of this, he concluded, "Although it is botched and patched up, it is the most worthy monument to be found in Rome, or, perhaps, anywhere else."

Architectural Challenges

AS IF Michelangelo had not been sufficiently busy, Pope Paul assigned him many architectural projects for the restoration and beautification of a despoiled city. In 1538, he asked the artist to redesign the Capitoline Hill of Rome, which had been for centuries the civic center of the city. Once glorious, the place had degenerated to the point that Emperor Charles V, while visiting two years earlier, had to take a detour around the hill to avoid the mud and spare the citizens a terrible embarrassment.

The two civic buildings on the hill—the Senate Building (Palazzo del Senatore), which was the seat of city government, and the Conservators' Palace (Palazzo dei Conservatori), the meeting place for the different guilds—were in bad shape and were positioned asymmetrically. A third building—the church of Santa Maria in Araceli—seemed out of place because it didn't look at all like the others. Michelangelo decided to work with the existing structure instead of fighting it.

Like all Renaissance artists, Michelangelo knew the importance of order, symmetry, and geometry. To give some coherence to that muddy mess, he started by marking the center of the area with an original statue of Emperor Marcus Aurelius which had been preserved in another area of town. Marcus Aurelius was still well respected as a wise philosopher king.

Once the center was marked, the artist worked on creating symmetry and order. He moved the Senate Building's bell tower to the center of the building and designed a new facade for the Conservators' Palace.

To balance the existing buildings, he designed a new construction (Palazzo Nuovo, or "New Palace") to flank the existing church. This new building mimics the Conservators' Palace and is positioned at the same 80-degree angle in reference to the Senate Building. Michelangelo unified the look of the three civic buildings by adding matching rectangular columns and decorative details. Besides giving a more uniform look, the columns work as focal points by attracting the eye to the orderliness of the place.

By their position, the three buildings create a trapezoidal space in front of them. In the Renaissance, the circle and the square were the most common architectural shapes, repre-

✛ **A view of the Capitoline Hill. From the left, Palazzo Nuovo, the Senate Building, and the Conservators' Palace.**
© iStock.com/lightkey

senting order and harmony. An oval, however, was the most logical complement to a trapezoidal space. Michelangelo used this shape as the outline of an elegant intersecting motif on the pavement, which pulls all the elements together, while giving a feeling of movement and encouraging the flow of visitors around the newly created piazza.

The slightly domed shape of the pavement accentuates the feeling of being on top of a hill—in fact, on the most prominent of Rome's seven hills. Much like in the Laurentian Library, a wide and elegant staircase, gentle enough to be mounted on horseback, encourages visitors to ascend to a quieter, more peaceful space. The staircase accentuates the central axis of the piazza and the symmetry of the buildings.

The Capitoline Hill was still incomplete when Michelangelo died. Tommaso de' Cavalieri took over control of the work, but many details were completed only much later. The pavement, for example, was finished in 1928.

St. Peter's Basilica

IN THE fall of 1546, Paul III approached the artist with a new assignment. The papal architect, Antonio da Sangallo the Younger, had just died, leaving the massive project of the rebuilding of St. Peter's Basilica unfinished. Paul III couldn't think of a better replacement than Michelangelo.

✛ **The pavement on the Capitoline Hill.**
Bruno, a.k.a. Pek, www.flickr.com/photos/_pek_/

As in most cases, Michelangelo tried to refuse. He was 71 years old, his health was deteriorating—especially his kidneys—and he already had more work than he could comfortably handle. He knew rebuilding St. Peter's had been a difficult venture and that his involvement in the work would generate some unpleasant opposition and resistance. Besides, it carried some painful personal memories—for years he had blamed Donato Bramante, the original architect of the reconstruction, for distracting Pope Julius from the building of the tomb.

CREATE A GEOMETRICAL PATTERN

YOU CAN CREATE a geometrical pattern with intersecting lines, similar to what Michelangelo did for the pavement on the Capitoline Hill.

Materials

✛ Drawing compass

✛ Paper

✛ Ruler

✛ Pencil with eraser to correct mistakes

✛ Colored pencils, markers, crayons, or paints (optional)

1. Place the spike of your compass in the center of your paper. The hole you are making will be your guide for the rest of the project. You may call it the "starting hole."

2. Open the compass to 4 inches (use your ruler to measure between the compass points if you need to). Turn the compass to draw a circle.

3. Select a point on the side of the circle and place the spike of your compass there.

4. Now place the pencil of the compass on the starting hole. Turn the compass to draw a circle.

5. Place the spike of your compass at one of the points where the two circles meet.

6. Place the pencil of the compass on the starting hole. Turn the compass to draw a circle.

7. Place the spike of your compass where the new circle meets the original one.

8. Place the pencil of the compass on the starting hole. Turn the compass to draw a circle.

9. Continue until you reach the last intersection.

10. Color your pattern however you like.

This pattern can be extended as much as you like. To continue, you can draw a thin line from

the center to the middle of two petals, place the spike of the compass there and the pencil of the compass in the starting hole, and then start a new series of circles.

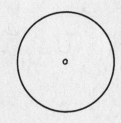
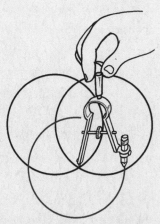

As he had done for other forms of art, he tried to persuade Pope Paul that architecture was not his trade, but his designs for the elegant Laurentian Library and the impressive Capitoline Hill proved the contrary. Finally, the artist accepted the assignment. "Pope Paul forced me against my will to work at St. Peter's," he wrote Vasari. On the other hand, the conditions of the contract were ideal, as Paul promised him "full, free, and complete permission and authority to change, refashion, enlarge, and contract the model and plan and the construction of the building as shall seem best to him." Michelangelo had the creative freedom he had always craved.

Even after 30 years of work, the area around St. Peter's was still a pitiful sight. With the old building left to deteriorate and the new building still covered by scaffolding and surrounded by rubble, the scene was far from the original vision of magnificence and awe.

Michelangelo recognized that Bramante—personal feelings aside—was a great architect. Bramante's successors, on the other hand, seemed so intent on adding and expanding that much of their construction had become an impediment rather than an improvement, detracting from the architectural clarity and light of the original. Besides, the projected expansion was so extensive that it might have required the destruction of the Pauline Chapel and maybe of the Sistine Chapel.

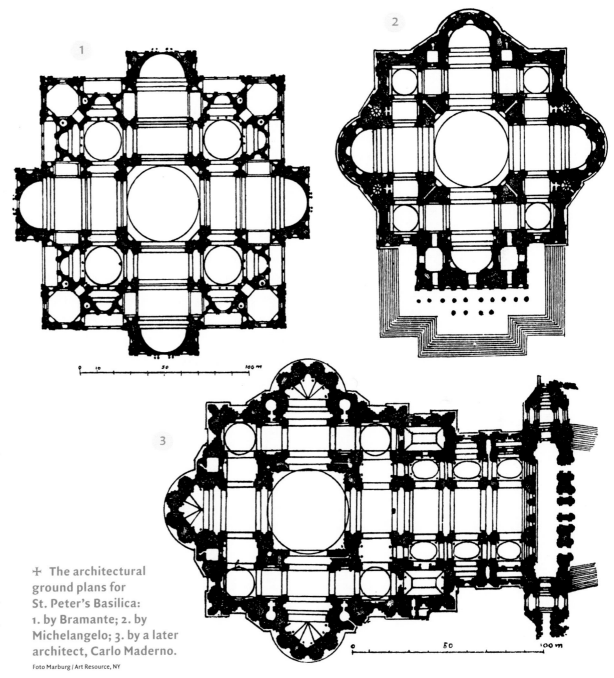

✢ The architectural ground plans for St. Peter's Basilica: 1. by Bramante; 2. by Michelangelo; 3. by a later architect, Carlo Maderno.

95

By accepting the commission, Michelangelo took on the colossal task of undoing years of architectural mistakes while relying on the help of a skeptical workforce that was still fervidly loyal to Sangallo. He went back to Bramante's original plan, making it even more compact and streamlined, and correcting some of its engineering defects. For example, he strengthened the parts of the structure that were clearly too weak to support the dome's weight.

Sangallo's model, which had cost 4,000 ducats, was discarded. Naturally, Sangallo's workers were outraged. They continued to express their remonstrance, especially after Pope Paul's death in November 1549. To their disappointment, the next pope, Julius III, confirmed Paul's promise to allow Michelangelo full creative freedom.

Michelangelo's most lasting contribution to the cathedral is the dome that crowns the building. The rest of the cathedral has been reworked throughout the centuries, and the final product looks somewhat different from what Michelangelo had planned.

Like Bramante, Michelangelo was inspired by the impressive dome Filippo Brunelleschi had designed in 1418 for the cathedral of Santa Maria del Fiore in Florence. To explain his idea for St. Peter's dome and to make sure it was preserved after his death, he built a model made of lime wood painted with tempera, which was about 15 times smaller than the original. The model was a cutaway, showing half of the dome, so the pope and his cardinals could see how he planned to build the inside portion.

Michelangelo copied Brunelleschi's plan of a double vault, with an internal dome inside an outer shell. He also took the idea of adding vertical ribs to the exterior dome, but he planned 16 where Brunelleschi had used eight. The ribs are both for decoration and strength. He added columns and a larger number of windows around the drum, as well as little windows on the cupola.

The dome was not yet built when Michelangelo died. Later architects modified his plan slightly by stretching the dome higher. This is actually an improvement, because the dome is now more visible than it would otherwise have been. In earlier drawings, Michelangelo had considered the possibility of such a change, so he would have most likely approved it.

The planning and oversight of St. Peter's occupied most of Michelangelo's later years. He often modified his plans in the course of the building, in an effort to get the building just right, just as a sculptor would continue to reshape the stone. For this reason, he refused other offers, including the insistent pleadings of Cosimo I, who continued to ask for his return to Florence.

He often felt conflicted. The duke's requests were very flattering. They also promised highest favors in the city the artist loved dearly, while the atmosphere at St. Peter's continued to be stressful and discouraging. Nevertheless, Michelangelo could not in good conscience leave the cathedral unless he knew it was in good hands. "I have always been, and still am, diligent," he explained to his nephew Lionardo, "because I believe, as many do, that I have been placed here by God."

✝ Michelangelo drew inspiration from the dome of the Santa Maria del Fiore in Florence (left), by architect Filippo Brunelleschi, for his design of St. Peter's Basilica dome (right). Jesus Taranchel Lopez / Pipopipo, Flickr

Other Architectural Works

AT HIS death, Sangallo left other buildings unfinished—particularly the Farnese Palace, residence of the pope's family and symbol of their power, and San Giovanni dei Fiorentini, a church designed for the Florentine population in Rome. Paul III asked Michelangelo to finish them.

Michelangelo displayed great abilities in working with existing structures and blending his style with Sangallo's, but he was also boldly innovative. For example, he was accused of breaking the rules of classical architecture when he made the last story of the Farnese Palace taller than the others. Michelangelo didn't care. Seen from ground level, the three stories appear to be equal, and that's what really mattered. "One should have compasses in one's eyes, not in one's hands," Michelangelo explained, "because the hands execute, but it is the eye that judges." He followed classical patterns not by reading manuals but by observing ancient buildings, which didn't always follow the rules.

Around the end of his life, Michelangelo designed two constructions for another pope, Pius IV: Porta Pia (a city gate) and the church of Santa Maria degli Angeli.

Pius IV wanted a city gate at the end of a long, scenic street (Via Pia), connecting his residence to the edge of Rome. Both the gate and the street bear the pope's name. In ancient Rome, city gates were used as means of defense, and their decorations expressed the city's awesomeness and power to outsiders.

By the time Michelangelo started to design the gate, however, it was obvious that city gates were not adequate means of defense. Besides, the pleasant nature of Via Pia required an equally attractive conclusion. Michelangelo planned a very elegant building and broke with tradition by placing the decorations on the in-

✛ **The church of Santa Maria degli Angeli in Rome.**

side. The gate then became a farewell sign for people leaving the city instead of a message to outsiders.

The adornments are also not warlike. In fact, he inserted some surprising elements, like the addition of two basins with towels—a supposed reminder of the pope's humble origins as a barber's son.

Today, Porta Pia is still very much as Michelangelo designed it. The only addition is the portion on top, which was added in the 19th century.

To build the church of Santa Maria degli Angeli, Michelangelo utilized an ancient Roman structure—one area of the public baths built by Emperor Diocletian between 298 and 306 CE. Visitors to the church are usually surprised when they go from the very plain facade, which still resembles a Roman ruin, to the spacious and luminous area inside. Even if today the church's interior hardly resembles Michelangelo's project, he was responsible for the overall idea. He also displayed engineering talent by raising the inside floor about six feet to protect the structure from humidity.

As an architect, Michelangelo continued to experiment with new styles and methods, finding new solutions to problems and joining his artistic talents with his innate engineering intuition. One of his most prominent skills was the talent to bring order and simplicity out of chaos, usually by finding the central

⚜ Public Baths in Ancient Rome ⚜

In ancient Rome, public baths were similar to today's spas. They were also important places of social gathering where lectures were held regularly. They were composed of several rooms, including bathing rooms, beauty salons, gyms, and swimming pools. The largest bathing structures included libraries, art museums, and shops. Servants were available to take care of the guests and provide massages and other services. The Baths of Diocletian were the largest in Rome and could hold up to 3,000 people.

Some of the rooms were named after the temperature of the water they provided. For example, the calidarium offered hot water (heated by a furnace placed under the floor), and the frigidarium, cold water. The church of Santa Maria degli Angeli was built inside the frigidarium of the Baths of Diocletian, which were the largest ever built in Roman times. The portion of the baths that is not occupied by the church is now a museum.

point of a structure and creating a symmetrical design around it.

Michelangelo never saw the completion of his architectural works but left some innovative projects and a great legacy to others. Later architects have learned from his courage to break with tradition without abandoning the fundamental and indispensable rules, his view of architecture as a dynamic and flexible art form, his attention to details and the meaning they can convey, and much more. In fact, some scholars believe Michelangelo's architectural innovations left a greater mark on later architects than his paintings and sculptures did on artists.

✠ THE ✠
LAST YEARS

The voyage of my life at last has reached ... the common port.

—MICHELANGELO, SONNET 285

A Mutilated Masterpiece

One evening in 1553, Giorgio Vasari stopped by Michelangelo's house to pick up a drawing for the pope. The house was dimly lit by a lamp. While Michelangelo's assistant Urbino went to get the drawing, Vasari noticed a large marble sculpture he had never seen before—a new pietà or, in this case, a scene of the removal of Jesus from the cross.

Before he could observe the details, Michelangelo dropped the lamp, plunging the room in total darkness. He then asked Urbino to bring another one. Turning to Vasari, he explained, "I am so old that oftentimes Death plucks me by the cape to go with him, and one day this body of mine will fall like the lantern, and the light of life will be put out."

Vasari realized that Michelangelo didn't want him to see the sculpture, at least not until it was finished. Today, the statue (often called *Florentine Pietà* because it is preserved in the museum of the Florentine cathedral of Santa Maria del Fiore) is not only unfinished but also mutilated.

Michelangelo began sculpting this statue in 1547 and intended it for his own grave. It represents a group of four people arranged in a pyramidal structure. Jesus is at the center, recently removed from the cross. At his right hand is his mother, Mary, who presses her body against him in an attempt to support him and seemingly become one with him. Her face is partially buried in his hair.

At Jesus's other side is his loyal follower Mary Magdalene, who, in the Bible, is the first person to talk to him after his resurrection. In the scene, she gently balances Mary's effort to support her son, while holding the sheet that would be used to wrap his body. Her sorrowful face turns away from him, inviting others to reflect on the scene.

Behind Jesus stands a large man who carries the bulk of his weight—Nicodemus, a teacher of Jewish law who became one of Jesus's secret followers. The Gospel of John tells how Nicodemus first approached Jesus by night for fear

✝ **Michelangelo's Florentine Pietà (also known as Pietà Bandini).** ©Vanni Archive / Art Resource

of the Jewish religious leaders, and engaged in a conversation with him about the kingdom of God. The same gospel describes him again after Jesus's death, when, together with another reputable Jew, he obtained permission to bury Jesus's body and prepared it for the burial.

The prominence of both Mary Magdalene and Nicodemus in a pietà is unusual, both in sculpture and in painting. Both of these figures had a strong significance for Michelangelo at this time. Mary Magdalene was traditionally seen as a remorseful sinner, and many of the artist's poems around this time were about repentance. As for Nicodemus—a man who had deep questions and kept his faith private, but revealed his devotion when most of Jesus's disciples had fled the scene—most experts agree Michelangelo chose this image to depict himself and his religious feelings.

This statue, the largest after the *David*, is one of the most challenging Michelangelo ever carved. Few sculptors had ever attempted to carve four figures from one single block of marble. In an art that is based on taking away rather than adding, a correction to one portion may affect other parts. In this composition, for example, Mary's face and left hand are probably left unfinished because refining those details would have damaged Jesus's already finished face and chest.

There is also a major flaw that casual viewers often fail to notice: Jesus is missing a leg. In the Florentine Cathedral, the statue is positioned in such a way that this detail might go unnoticed, and most photographers avoid taking pictures of the damaged area. From the right side of the statue, however, the mutilation is obvious. In Jesus's pelvis, there is a hole carved by a later sculptor to allow for the addition of an attachment.

Biographers are unsure why Michelangelo abandoned this project. Vasari suggested the marble may have been flawed or too hard, but by this time Michelangelo would have recognized a faulty block from the start. As for hard marble, it had never stopped the artist before.

Even his aging doesn't seem a plausible reason. Just a few years earlier, a visitor had commented:

I am able to affirm that have seen Michelangelo, at the age of more than sixty years and not the strongest for his time of life, knock off more chips from an extremely hard marble in a quarter of an hour than three young stone-cutters could have done in three or four—a thing quite incredible thing to one who has not seen it. He put such impetuosity and fury into his work, that I thought the whole must fly to pieces; hurling to the ground in one blow great fragments three or four inches thick, shaving the line so closely, that if he had overpassed it by a hair's-breadth he ran the risk of losing all, since one cannot mend a marble afterwards or repair mistakes, as one does with figures of clay and stucco.

✝ **Giorgio Vasari, Michelangelo's friend, fellow artist, and biographer.**

Ex S.S.P.S.A.E and for the Polo Museale of the City of Florence—Gabinetto Fotografico

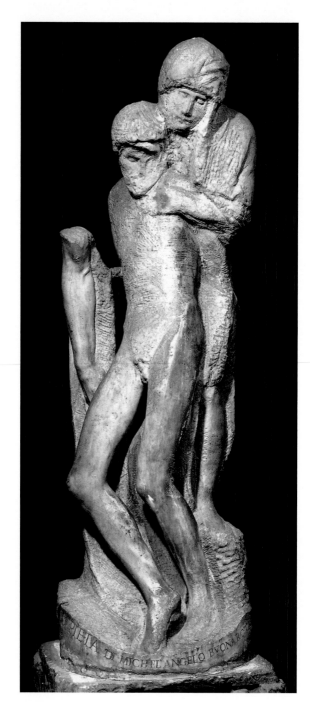

This time the challenge might have been too difficult even for Michelangelo. To him, adding a leg from another piece of marble would have been inadmissible, and shaping a new leg in the same block of marble would have caused the elimination of other important features, if not the reworking of the whole sculpture.

In addition, Michelangelo had increasingly felt that depicting divine subjects was futile and even dangerous, as he expressed in a poem:

In such slavery, and with so much weariness,
and with false conceptions and great peril
to my soul, to be here sculpting divine things.

In the end, Michelangelo let his pupil Tiberio Calcagni restore the piece, then gave the statue to a friend. Calcagni might have tried to repair the leg and probably finished the image of Mary Magdalene. In any case, this statue is still hailed as a masterpiece.

The Last Pietà

IN SPITE of these problems, Michelangelo continued to use sculpture, drawings, and poetry as means to explore and express his feelings about religion, especially Jesus's crucifixion and removal from the cross. He experimented with different poses and feelings. An important sculpture portraying these feelings is the *Rondanini Pietà*.

Like Michelangelo's first pietà, this one depicts only Mary and her son. It is, however, completely different. In fact, it is different from anything he had ever made, including the *Florentine Pietà*.

The first *Pietà*, sculpted 60 years earlier, is a refined masterpiece of classical art, emphasizing perfection and beauty. This last one is unfinished and resembles a modern sculpture, where forms are only means of expressing concepts and feelings. The first *Pietà* is a proud work, confidently signed by the young artist. The last one is a humble and hesitant meditation on approaching death.

It's obvious that Michelangelo reworked the statue many times, as both figures are very thin and bear signs of many transformations. The most obvious result of this reworking is Jesus's detached right arm, which stands suspended separate from the body. If the arm had been finished, the shoulder would end up near his head. Michelangelo must have started a larger statue and then resculpted the heads of Jesus and Mary. It's interesting that Michelangelo never removed the first arm.

Today, both faces are still rough, and one of Mary's hands is so thin from alterations that it almost sinks into her son's body in an insufficient attempt to sustain its weight. In fact, it looks as if Jesus is supporting Mary, who stands on a rock behind him. As it is today, this statue is considered one of the most moving sculptures the artist ever created.

The Shadow of Death

FOR YEARS, Michelangelo had been aware that his life was nearing its end, a realization compounded by the death of friends and relatives. One of the most painful departures was the unexpected death of Vittoria Colonna in 1547. "[She] loved me very much, and I loved her no less," he wrote. "Death deprived me of a great friend." In fact, Michelangelo had never found in anyone else the same religious and poetic like-mindedness he enjoyed with Colonna. To this "high and godly lady" he could freely and humbly confide the deepest uncertainties of his soul, always receiving in return comfort and wisdom.

Michelangelo mourned her death for months, cherishing a collection of her poems she had given him as a present. Over the last few years, the two had planned to publish his poems too, but her death had stanched this desire.

The loss of Colonna was followed by the death of Michelangelo's brother Giovan Simone in 1548, and the death of Paul III—Michelangelo's greatest patron—in 1549. By that time, Michelangelo had already outlived many of his friends.

Some other friends had left Italy for religious reasons. In 1547, a major church council, meeting in the northern city of Trent, marked a final separation between Roman Catholics and Protestants by declaring officially cursed (anathema) the doctrine of salvation through faith alone. The religious climate in Italy changed almost overnight.

More than ever before, the Spirituali had to choose between leaving the country, keeping secret convictions, or facing death. Things became worse in 1555, when Cardinal Gian Pietro Carafa, an archenemy of Protestants and the motor behind the reinstitution of the Roman **Inquisition**, became pope with the name of Paul IV.

With the changing tides, some of the Spirituali were imprisoned on suspicion of Lutheran **heresy**, while others left the country. Michelangelo lamented their absence in his letters and poems. In 1557, a major trial against one of the Spirituali brought to light many names and connections, creating a climate of fear.

Unlike his predecessors, Pope Paul IV didn't assign any new tasks to Michelangelo. In fact, one of his first acts was cutting off the artist's pension. By this time, however, Michelangelo didn't need any additional income. He could live very comfortably on the money he had saved.

Michelangelo suffered another painful blow in 1556, with the death of Urbino, his close

✛ A charcoal drawing of Michelangelo in his old age, by his friend Daniele da Volterra, who was hired to cover up some of the nudity in Michelangelo's *The Last Judgment*. Wikimedia Commons

friend and faithful caretaker. "I can barely write," he told Vasari. "You know Urbino is dead. He has been a great gift of God to me but has also caused me great hurt and infinite sorrow. The gift is this: while living, he kept me alive, and with his death he taught me to die, not unwillingly, but with yearning."

As godfather of Urbino's children, the artist provided for them and their mother, Cornelia, until he died. He was especially close to the youngest, who bore his name.

Loneliness, frequent illnesses, and old age weighed heavily on Michelangelo, who expressed his weariness in one of his longest poems.

I am shut up here, all alone and poor,
as is the pulp of a fruit by its husk,
like a genie bound up in a bottle.

After a long and dismal description of his bodily ills—including agonizing kidney stones and frequent respiratory trouble—he described his gloomy appearance:

My face has a shape that's enough to terrify;
my clothes could chase crows, with no further rags,
away from fresh, dry seed and into the wind.

In one of my ears a spider web is nestled,
and in the other a cricket sings all night;
my raspy breath keeps me from sleeping or snoring.

Even his art seemed useless. In his view, his papers full of sketches or writings were good only to be used as "tambourines and wrappings," if not for worse purposes. His sculptures looked like puppets, he said, or "playthings."

Hope for an Heir

ONE OF Michelangelo's hopes was the preservation of the Buonarroti name. He had never married, which was not unusual for artists in those days. In his biography, he explained that art was his wife and his works were his children. Near the end of his life, however, when his nephew Lionardo was the only hope for the perpetuation of the family name, Michelangelo spent much time giving him advice on how to find a proper wife.

Nobility was important, since the Buonarroti family was, at least in Michelangelo's eyes, an ancient and noble Florentine family. With the artist's financial help, Lionardo didn't have to worry about receiving a dowry. "I think there must be in Florence many noble families who are also poor," Michelangelo wrote, and poverty might be an actual asset, because "they would not be overly proud." Besides a noble lineage, other qualities were "health and especially goodness. Don't worry too much about beauty," the artist told the nephew, "since you are not the handsomest man in Florence."

As time went by, Michelangelo started to lose hope. In 1553, his 35-year old nephew was still spending much of his time looking for fun, often with questionable companions. The artist gave him an ultimatum. If Lionardo didn't act quickly, Michelangelo was ready to leave his fortune to orphanages and hospitals and to ask his nephew for a repayment for all the benefits he had given him throughout his life.

The threat seemed effective, because the same year, Lionardo married a girl from a reputable family, Cassandra Ridolfi. Overjoyed, Michelangelo sent her two rings—one with a diamond and one with a ruby. From then on, in every letter to his nephew, he invariably sent some expressions of gratitude to Cassandra.

Lionardo seemed very happy with his wife. "We have to thank [God] for it, especially because it's a rare thing," Michelangelo wrote.

The artist was thrilled at the birth of their first child, Buonarroto. After him, they had other children, but three died in infancy. With each death, Michelangelo expressed both sorrow and resignation: "This is our lot: our family can't multiply in Florence."

Lionardo and Cassandra had another boy four years after Michelangelo's death, and named him after the artist. Michelangelo the Younger became a famous writer and playwright and was the first editor of his great-uncle's poetry.

Death of Michelangelo

IN SPITE of aging, Michelangelo remained active, walking or riding his horse almost every day until the end of his life. Horseback riding was considered a healthy activity at that time. One of his most frustrating ailments must have been his hand cramps, which prevented him from writing. Around the end of his life, many of his letters were dictated to an assistant. Mentally, however, he was as sharp as ever.

In February 1564, he was struck by a fever. Instead of resting in bed, however, he went out for a walk in the rain. When his assistant Calcagni tried to bring him back home, Michelangelo replied, "What do you want me to do? I am ill and I can't find peace anywhere." Alarmed, Calcagni informed Lionardo immediately.

That night, Michelangelo was unable to sleep and tried again to go out, but his weakness forced him to sit back in his chair in front of the fire, which he preferred to his bed. The news of his illness spread, and his friends, including Tommaso de' Cavalieri, gathered around him to assist him.

He was visited by two doctors who prescribed a great variety of medicines, from sweetened water with sage to crushed pearl in rose water—the same remedy that was prescribed for Lorenzo de' Medici on his deathbed. On

✠ A statue of Michelangelo the Younger, the artist's grandnephew, by Giuliano Finelli.
Scala / Art Resource, NY

Michelangelo's instructions, his friends read to him Bible passages on the sufferings and death of Jesus.

On February 17, as Michelangelo's condition worsened, Calcagni urged Lionardo to hurry. "We expect that your Michelangelo wants to leave us for good," he wrote, but Lionardo couldn't arrive in time. Michelangelo died the following evening, just two weeks before his 89th birthday.

The next day, a judge and a notary came to make an inventory of Michelangelo's belongings. The five-page inventory listed all his furniture and his clothes, mostly black—a color of nobility. These included two fur coats and two cloaks, two black hats, and a pair of slippers. Coins, in various currencies, were hidden everywhere—in pots, vases, old sacks, and inside knotted handkerchiefs. The total sum was enough to build a small building. This was only a small portion of the artist's riches, which included bank accounts and several properties.

Grave Robbers

LIONARDO ARRIVED three days after Michelangelo's death and took care of the final arrangements. He realized that a few items had been stolen. There were also some missing drawings, but it's possible that Michelangelo had burned them before he died.

Soon after the artist's death, his body was carried in a solemn and well-attended procession to the nearby Church of the Twelve Holy Apostles while Pope Pius declared his intentions of building a suitable tomb for Michelangelo in the St. Peter's Basilica. On the other hand, Lionardo knew his uncle wanted to be

---

MAKE AUTHENTIC GARLIC BREAD

IN ITALY, garlic bread is a traditional "peasant food," as it makes use of stale bread. Michelangelo was the equivalent of a millionaire today, but he lived very frugally, so he probably enjoyed garlic bread on several occasions. In Tuscany, it is called *fettunta*.

Serves 2–4 people

Materials
+ 4 slices of Italian bread
+ Toaster
+ Plate
+ 1 clove of garlic, peeled and cut in half
+ 4 teaspoons olive oil (or more, if desired)
+ Salt

1. Place the slices in a toaster and cook until slightly brown.

2. While the bread is still warm but not too hot to touch, place the slices on a plate.

3. Hold a slice in one hand and rub the garlic all over the bread with your other hand. Do the same for all four slices.

4. Pour a teaspoon of olive oil on each slice, tilting the slices so that the oil spreads evenly.

5. Sprinkle some salt on each slice.

6. Enjoy by itself or with a meal.

buried in Florence, and one of Michelangelo's friends confirmed the artist had expressed the same wish two days before dying.

Fearing complications, Lionardo arranged a secret removal. The next Saturday, after sunrise, a cart pulled into the cloister of the church, and Michelangelo's body, wrapped in cloth, was hidden among other large bundles. The driver was a well-known merchant who took frequent trips to Rome, so no one suspected him as he left the city. The trip was long, with frequent pauses and maybe a change of mules. Lionardo had paid everything in advance, including a generous sum to the driver and another fee to a soldier who waited for the cart outside Rome and escorted it to Florence.

On March 11, three weeks after Michelangelo's death, the cart arrived at one of Florence's city gates, where Vasari took charge. The escorts were glad to get rid of the uncomfortable bundle. Immediately, the cart driver went to an inn to get drunk; he promised to go to church to confess his sins the following day.

The body was temporarily placed in the church of San Pier Maggiore, until a group of Florentine artists came to escort the coffin in a torchlight procession to Santa Croce—the same church the artist had attended as a child. Vasari had hoped to keep the transport fairly private, but word got out. In the end, so many

❧ Medicine in Michelangelo's Time ❧

In the Renaissance, medicine was still largely based on the ancient theory that human health is influenced by four bodily fluids (known as humors): blood, yellow bile, black bile, and phlegm. In nature, they corresponded to the elements of air, fire, water, and earth. To be healthy, a person had to find harmony between these humors by combining the right foods, avoiding extreme weather conditions, and moderating emotions. The idea of germs as carriers of illnesses was just being developed.

For example, Lodovico once suggested Michelangelo's stomach troubles might be the effect of "discomforts, fatigue, the choice of bad or windy foods, cold to the feet, or wetness." He added a remedy he had used: "For several days, I ate only boiled bread, chicken, or eggs, taking some **cassia** by mouth. I also made a paste with ground marinated fava beans, incense, mashed and dried rose petals, and saffron, and mixed them in a small pot with oils of rose and chamomile." Lodovico applied the paste to his stomach and belly, and healed "in a few days."

Some remedies sound particularly strange to modern readers. When Urbino became ill, the doctor prescribed a large number of syrups and medicines, including gold-plated pills (because gold, being a precious metal, was considered very healthful). Other unusual ingredients included fox oil and powdered antlers. It's not surprising that Michelangelo once said, "I believe more in prayers than in medicine."

people crowded Santa Croce that it was difficult to move the coffin around.

Duke Cosimo honored the artist on July 14 by holding an expensive and impressive memorial at the church of San Lorenzo. There, the coffin was placed on an elegant platform and surrounded by paintings provided by the best artists of Florence. A series of these paintings

✛ Grandduke Cosimo I de' Medici, by Agnolo Bronzino, c. 1545. Erich Lessing / Art Resource, NY

portrayed the main events of Michelangelo's life, including his first encounter with Lorenzo de' Medici.

Michelangelo's life had come full circle as his body returned to the places where his artistic life had taken wings. The skinny but confident young boy, eager to win the Medici's favor, was an image of the past. The tables had turned, and Duke Cosimo was now eager to turn some rays of Michelangelo's glory on the Medici family and on the city the artist had never ceased to love.

Michelangelo had never been the lowly workman his father had feared he would become. He had lived his life as a gentleman as much as an artist—proudly upholding his noble lineage and fiercely defending his talents and artistic intuitions as gifts given by God for a divinely ordained purpose.

He has been called both divine and tormented. He has been acclaimed as an artistic giant and "more than a mortal." A novel and a movie have celebrated his agony and his ecstasy, and his works still leave us astonished. His adventurous life, often caught in the entanglements, power struggles, and religious upheavals of the 16th century, has all the ingredients for an exciting action movie.

Yet, Michelangelo's life was not just one blaze of excitement. Most of his 89 years were characterized by long days of meticulous and patient work—yielding to fickle popes, teaching mediocre students, discarding ruined blocks of stone, sharpening tools, and beating his chisel, day in and day out. All of these things combined to mature him as an artist and as a man, and to make his works powerful and timeless.

ACKNOWLEDGMENTS

First of all, I'd like to thank my editor, Lisa Reardon, who suggested this title in the first place. This book may not have come into being without her encouragement; Lisa has been a pillar of support, patiently providing guidance and direction. Thanks also to my friend and fellow author Nancy Sanders, who helped me make the initial decision to pursue this project, and to the editors and artists at Chicago Review Press, who have done an impressive, highly professional job.

I am deeply indebted to Dr. William E. Wallace; Barbara Murphy Bryant, distinguished professor of art history at Columbia University and author of several books, lectures, and articles on Michelangelo; Dr. John T. Spike, distinguished scholar in residence at the College of William and Mary in Williamsburg, Virginia, and author of *Young Michelangelo: The Path to the Sistine*; and Victor Coonin, James F. Ruffin Professor of Art History at Rhodes College and author of *From Marble to Flesh: The Biography of Michelangelo's "David"* for answering my frequent questions. Dr. Spike and Prof. Coonin have also read one of my chapters and have offered valuable insights.

I am also grateful to Dr. Antonio Forcellino, art restorer and author of *Michelangelo: A Tormented Life*, who has kindly taken the time to read my manuscript and answer my questions. Heartfelt thanks to my friends Heather Chait-Chisholm, Timothy Massaro, Ellie Charter, and Dianna Ippolito for their patient reading of my manuscript and their helpful suggestions.

I couldn't have done without the help of many families who have tested the activities in this book: the Richards, the Plotners, the Sanchezes, the Van Bibbers, and the Pisanis. At times, I felt we were all sitting at one big table having fun together.

Finally, thanks to my husband, Tom, who has encouraged me from start to finish.

GLOSSARY

aqueduct A man-made structure or channel that carries water, usually to a city.

anatomy The study of the structure of organisms.

apostle In the Bible, each of the twelve men commissioned by Jesus to spread his message and build and strengthen the first Christian churches. The word also has a more generic meaning of "messenger."

barge A flat-bottomed boat for carrying goods, especially by river.

bas-relief A type of sculpture in which the figures are only slightly more raised than the background.

bastion A type of protective fortification thrusting out at an angle from a wall.

buttress A structure of stone built against a wall.

contrapposto An artistic technique, invented by the Greeks, in which a human figure stands with most of its weight on one foot, to suggest relaxation and/or activity.

cassia *Cassia fistula*. A tropical tree used for ornamental and medicinal purposes.

centaur A creature in Greek mythology that is half human and half horse.

Christendom In a general sense, the word means the collective body of Christians throughout the world. The "rise of Christendom" indicates the growth of a Christian geographical and political society in the Middle Ages that sought to embed Christian beliefs and practices in society at large.

clergy The group of officials who are ordained for religious duties, especially in the Christian church.

cloister A covered walk in a convent, monastery, or church.

cross-hatch In art, to mark with a pattern of crossing fine lines.

cupid A representation of a winged, naked child with bow and arrow that portrays the Roman god of love, Cupid.

dapple Spotted.

dowry In some cultures, property or money a bride brings to her husband when they marry.

ducat Golden or silver coin, originated in Venice and later used in many European countries.

duchy A region under the rule of a duke or duchess.

excommunicate To deny church membership and participation in the sacraments.

facade The face or front of a building.

florin A golden coin, issued for the first time in Florence in 1252.

foster-mother A woman providing the care a mother usually gives to a child.

friar A member of a Roman Catholic religious order for men.

fresco A painting technique that involves painting on wet plaster, the most common technique used in the Renaissance for painting walls and ceilings.

gonfaloniere The highest position in Florence's republic.

gospel Literally meaning "good news," the Christian message of salvation from God's judgment of sin through Christ's life, death, and resurrection.

guild City corporation controlling the arts and trade.

heresy A religious opinion that contradicts the most basic doctrines of a church.

Inquisition A Roman Catholic tribunal originally established by Pope Gregory IX in 1231 to suppress views that were contrary to those held by the church. It was brought back in 1542 by Cardinal Carafa with a specific focus on the suppression of Lutheran teachings.

intoxication The condition of being drunk.

lantern In architecture, a structure on top of a roof that lets air and/or light into a building.

lapis lazuli A deep blue stone used in decoration and jewelry, or when finely crushed, as pigment for painting.

mass Religious service of the Roman Catholic Church.

mausoleum A building housing one or more tombs.

mediator A person who helps two or more people reconcile or resolve differences.

mythology A set of stories and traditions related to a particular culture or time.

patron A generous supporter, who usually provides financial gifts to an artist.

piazza A town square.

pietà Italian for "pity." In art, the word is used to indicate a scene with Mary mourning the death of her son Jesus and holding his body.

pigment A natural substance used for coloring and painting.

plague An epidemic disease causing a high rate of death. The word can be used to describe a specific disease (such as the bubonic plague), but in the Middle Ages and Renaissance it was often used in a generic sense.

plaster A soft mixture of lime, water, and sand or cement, that is applied to walls and ceilings and becomes hard and smooth when dry.

pope The head of the Roman Catholic Church.

prior The head of a religious house for monks or friars.

quarry A place where building stones are extracted.

quill A pen made from a feather.

republic A government ruled by elected representatives.

satyr A mythological lesser god who lived in the woods. The Greeks represented him as a man with a horse's ears and tail and the Romans as a man with a goat's ears, tail, legs, and horns.

scaffold A temporary structure used as support during a building or artistic project.

sfumato A technique of letting colors blend naturally together, producing soft and vague outlines.

sibyl For the ancient Greeks, a woman who could receive messages from a god.

stencil A sheet of cardboard, plastic, or metal used to reproduce a pattern on another sheet by tracing the outline or by applying ink, paint, or charcoal through holes.

stonemason A skilled tradesperson who works with stone.

stylus An instrument used to write on clay or wax. Fresco artists used it to mark the outlines of their drawings on plaster.

terra-cotta A type of clay that turns reddish when baked.

theologian A person who studies God and religion.

theological Related to the study of God and religion.

Tuscan Relating to the Italian region of Tuscany.

wet nurse A woman hired to breastfeed and care for a child.

KEY FIGURES

Ammannati, Bartolommeo (1511–1592) Artist and friend of Michelangelo. He contributed to the completion of the Medici Chapel and the Laurentian Library, especially the staircase.

Adrian VI (1459–1523) Adrian Florensz. He became pope in 1522.

Alexander VI (1431–1503) Rodrigo Borgia of Valencia. He became pope in 1492 and was known as a ruthless leader who allowed his son Cesare Borgia to rule Rome with terror and cruelty.

Aldrovandi, Giovan Francesco (d. 1512) Member of a prominent Bolognese family. He was a patron of Michelangelo from 1494 to 1495.

Alighieri, Dante (c. 1265–c. 1320) Poet and political thinker who had a great influence on Michelangelo. His greatest work is *The Divine Comedy*, a long epic poem in three books (*Inferno*, *Purgatorio*, and *Paradiso*).

Argenta, Piero d' (d. 1529) Michelangelo's student and assistant.

Bayezid II (1447–1512) Sultan of the Ottoman Empire. He invited Michelangelo to build a bridge over the Bosporus.

Boccaccio, Giovanni (1313–1375) Author of popular works, especially *The Decameron*, in which he denounced the corruption and hypocrisy of his times.

Bramante, Donato (1444–1514) Julius II's main architect. He drew plans for the complete rebuilding of St. Peter's Basilica.

Brunelleschi, Filippo (1337–1446) Florentine architect and sculptor. He is considered the founder of Renaissance architecture. His greatest work is the dome of the Cathedral of Florence.

Buonarroti, Buonarroto (1477–1528) Michelangelo's second and closest brother. He died from the plague. He had three children: Lionardo, Simone, and Francesca.

Buonarroti Francesca (1519–1578) Eldest child of Buonarroto. After her father's death in 1528, Michelangelo placed her under the care

of the nuns at the convent in Boldrone, Florence, until she married Michele Guicciardini in 1537.

Buonarroti, Giovan Simone (1479–1548) Michelangelo's third brother.

Buonarroti, Gismondo (1481–1555) Michelangelo's youngest brother.

Buonarroti, Leonardo (1473–c. 1510) Michelangelo's oldest brother. He became a Dominican friar.

Buonarroti, Lionardo (1522–1599) Second child and eldest son of Buonarroto. He became Michelangelo's heir.

Buonarroti, Lodovico (1444–1534) Michelangelo's father. He came from a wealthy family of merchants who lost much money over time. He held a few modest jobs for the Medici government. Soon after his wife Francesca died, he married Lucrezia Ubaldini. Michelangelo never talked about his stepmother.

Buonarroti, Simone (1526–1530) Third child of Buonarroto. He died of unknown causes.

Calcagni, Tiberio (b. 1532) Sculptor and architect. He was Michelangelo's pupil and assistant.

Cavalieri, Tommaso de' (d. 1587) Roman nobleman. He was one of Michelangelo's closest friends in the 1530s. He was present at the artist's death.

Clement VII (1478–1534) Giulio de' Medici. Son of Giuliano and nephew of Lorenzo the Magnificent. He became pope in 1523 and was one of Michelangelo's most appreciative patrons.

Colonna, Vittoria (1490–1547) Marchesa di Pescara. She was an influential poet of her time and a close friend of Michelangelo from about 1537 until her death.

Condivi, Ascanio (c. 1525–1574) Michelangelo's friend, pupil, and assistant. He wrote *Life of Michelangelo* under the artist's supervision (published in 1553).

Donatello di Niccolò di Betto Bardi (1386–1466) Sculptor, known simply as Donatello. He developed a style of realistic and highly emotional sculptures. He is considered second to Michelangelo as the best Italian sculptor of the Renaissance.

Este, Alfonso d' (1476–1534) Duke of Ferrara from 1504 to his death. Michelangelo visited his court to receive his military advice.

Galli, Iacopo (d. 1505) Riario's banker and Michelangelo's patron.

Giotto di Bondone (1266/7–1337) A revolutionary painter who adopted a scientific approach to perspective, breaking with the medieval tradition of flat, unexpressive figures and creating realistic scenes.

Ghirlandaio, Domenico (1449–1494) Renowned Florentine painter who employed Michelangelo in his workshop.

Giovanni, Bertoldo di (c. 1420–1491) Sculptor and medalist who trained Michelangelo in the Medici court.

Granacci, Francesco (1469–1543) Painter. He studied with Michelangelo under Domenico Ghirlandaio.

Guicciardini, Michele (d. 1553) Nobleman, husband of Michelangelo's niece Francesca Buonarroti.

Julius II (1443–1513) Giuliano della Rovere. Nicknamed "the Warrior Pope," he was the first pope to employ Michelangelo. He commissioned a tomb, a bronze statue in Bologna, and the ceiling of the Sistine Chapel.

Julius III (1487–1555) Giovanni Maria Ciocchi. He became pope in 1550 and renewed Michelangelo's position as supreme architect of St. Peter's.

Leo X (1475–1521) Giovanni de' Medici. Second son of Lorenzo the Magnificent. He became pope in 1521 and commissioned the facade of San Lorenzo in Florence.

Maderno, Carlo (1556–1629) Swiss Italian architect. He drew new plans for St. Peter's and finished its facade after Michelangelo's death.

"Masaccio," Tommaso Cassai (1401–1428/9) Painter. He developed Giotto's method of creating a greater sense of three-dimensional space.

Medici, Alessandro de' (1511–1537) Became Duke of Florence in 1532.

Medici, Cosimo de' (b. 1519) He became Duke of Florence in 1537 and Grand Duke of Tuscany in 1569.

Medici, Giuliano de' (1453–1478) Brother of Lorenzo the Magnificent and coruler of Florence.

Medici, Giuliano de' (1478–1518) Duke of Nemours.

Medici, Lorenzo de' (1492–1519) Duke of Urbino.

Medici, Lorenzo de' (the Magnificent) (1449–1492) Head of the Medici family and lover of arts. He ruled Florence from 1469 until his death.

Medici, Lorenzo di Pierfrancesco de' (1463–1503) Florentine banker and politician who helped Michelangelo on his return to Florence.

Medici, Piero de' (the Fatuous) (1472–1503) First son of Lorenzo the Magnificent. He ruled Florence from 1492 until his exile in 1494.

Mona Margherita (d. 1540) Longtime servant of the Buonarroti family.

Neri, Francesca de' (d. 1497) Michelangelo's mother.

Paul III (1468–1549) Alessandro Farnese. He became pope in 1534 and commissioned the *Last Judgment*, the Pauline Chapel, St. Peter's Basilica, and the Farnese Palace.

Paul IV (1476–1559) Giampietro Carafa. He became pope in 1555 and was determined to cleanse the church of Protestant teachings.

Petrarch (Francesco Petrarca, 1304–1374) Major exponent of a new style of poetry ("Dolce Stil Novo") that emphasized platonic love, idealized beauty, and the use of metaphors and introspection.

Pius III (1439–1503) Francesco Piccolomini. He was pope for only 26 days after Alexander VI. He died of an ulcer in his leg. Some think he was poisoned.

Pius IV (1499–1565) Giovanni Angelo de' Medici. He became pope in 1559. He asked Michelangelo to design Porta Pia and Santa Maria degli Angeli.

Poliziano, Angelo (1454–1494) One of the most important poets of the Renaissance.

Raphael (Raffaello Sanzio) (1483–1520) Painter and architect known for his delicate images.

Riario, Raffaele (1461–1521) Cardinal and lover of the arts. He commissioned the statue of Bacchus from Michelangelo and allowed him to become established in Rome.

Ridolfi, Cassandra (d. 1593) Wife of Lionardo Buonarroti.

Sangallo, Antonio da, the Younger (1484–1546) Papal architect. Michelangelo took his place in designing St. Peter's Basilica, the Farnese Palace, and the church of San Giovanni dei Fiorentini.

"Topolino," Domenico di Giovanni di Bertino Fancelli (b. 1464) Stonecarver and quarry supervisor from Settignano, and longtime assistant of Michelangelo.

Torrigiano, Pietro (1472–1528) Sculptor who studied under Bertoldo di Giovanni. He was responsible for breaking Michelangelo's nose in a fight. He became influential in introducing the Renaissance to England. He later moved to Spain, where an angry outburst led him to be accused of heresy and condemned by the Spanish Inquisition. He died after starving himself in prison.

Savonarola, Girolamo (1452–1498) Dominican friar who opposed the corruption of both church and government. He contributed to establishing the Florentine republic after the departure of Piero de' Medici. His constant attacks against the pope led to his excommunication and final execution.

Soderini, Piero (1450–1522) Politician. He became head of the Republic of Florence.

"Urbino" Francesco di Bernardino Amadori (d. 1556) Artist and pupil of Michelangelo. He was Michelangelo's closest friend from about 1530 until Urbino's death. After that, Michelangelo provided for Urbino's wife, Cornelia, and their two sons.

Vasari, Giorgio (1511–1574) Painter and architect. He was the author of *Lives of the Most Excellent Painters, Sculptors, and Architects*, first published in 1550, including a biography of Michelangelo. The book was revised and expanded in a 1568 edition. Vasari completed Michelangelo's work in the Laurentian Library.

Vinci, Leonardo da (1452–1519) Florentine painter, who also created important works as an architect, a musician, a writer, and an inventor. Michelangelo saw him as a rival.

Volterra, Daniele da (1509–1566) Sculptor, painter, and friend of Michelangelo. He is remembered for painting clothes on Michelangelo's nudes in *The Last Judgment*.

RESOURCES TO EXPLORE

 ## Websites

Michelangelo: The Complete Works
www.michelangelo-gallery.org
A large part of Michelangelo's works can be viewed individually or in a slide show.

Vatican Open Tours
http://vatican.com/tour
Take a virtual tour of the Sistine Chapel. You can explore on your own, or choose the guided tour. The site has also a virtual tour of St. Peter's Square.

Vatican Virtual Tour
www.vatican.va/various/cappelle/sistina_vr
  /index.html
Click on the links for a virtual tour of the Sistine Chapel, the Pauline Chapel, and St. Peter's.

Accademia Gallery in Florence: The Life of Michelangelo
www.accademia.org/michelangelo
Read about Michelangelo's life, or click on "Explore the Museum—The Artworks" to read more about Michelangelo's *David* and his four Slaves.

The Museums in Florence
www.museumsinflorence.com/musei
  /Laurentian_Library.html
Read about the Laurentian Library and view photos of the place and some of its ancient and valuable books.

The British Museum: Teachers' Guide for the BP Special Exhibition *Michelangelo Drawings: Closer to the Master*

www.britishmuseum.org/PDF/british_museum
_michelangelo_drawings.pdf

A very useful teacher's guide, full of interesting suggestions, activities, and probing questions. It provides an opportunity to discover more about Michelangelo and his art.

Puzzles-Games.eu

http://puzzles-games.eu/search.html?search
_keywords=michelangelo

Enjoy some puzzles of Michelangelo's paintings.

Web Gallery of Art: Michelangelo

www.wga.hu/index1.html

View a fairly complete collection of Michelangelo's works.

Web Gallery of Art: Sistine Chapel Ceiling

www.wga.hu/tours/sistina/index1.html

Click on the different portions of the fresco to find out what Michelangelo painted and why.

Life of Michelangelo

http://easyweb.easynet.co.uk/giorgio.vasari
/michel/michel.htm

Another collection of works by Michelangelo, arranged in chronological order, with comments by Vasari.

Artcyclopedia

www.artcyclopedia.com/artists/michelangelo
_buonarroti.html

Explore some useful links to museums, public websites, and art databases.

Michelangelo

www.michelangelo.com/buon/bio-index2.html

A brief account of Michelangelo's life, with some links to other sites.

Videos

***The Divine Michelangelo.* Produced and directed by Tim Dunn and Stuart Elliott. BBC, 2004.**

www.youtube.com/watch?v=iK6MC7EZhys&
list=PL9ACCB2D2A1D856E8

An exciting recounting of Michelangelo's life, with comments from experts. There is one rather gruesome scene in which Michelangelo dissects a cadaver.

Wallace, William E. *The Genius of Michelangelo.* The Great Courses. DVD. The Teaching Company, 2007.

A serious and detailed study for older children and adults who want to explore all aspects of Michelangelo's life and work.

Books

Di Cagno, Gabriella. *Michelangelo: Master of the Italian Renaissance.* Illustrations by Simone Boni. New York: Peter Bedrick Books, 2001.

Grades 6–12. An accurate and clear overview of the artist, his times, and his works.

NOTES

When only an Italian source is referenced, the text was translated by the author from the original Italian.

Introduction

"Enough, enough, enough!": Mark Twain, *The Innocents Abroad, or The New Pilgrim's Progress* (San Francisco: Bancroft,1869; Project Gutenberg), www.gutenberg.org/files/3176/3176-h/3176-h.htm, quoted in Wallace, *The Genius of Michelangelo*, DVD.

"by the brush": Vasari, *Lives of the Most Eminent Painters, Sculptors and Architects*, section 5.

Chapter 1

"Beauty I was given": Buonarroti, *Le rime di Michelangelo Buonarroti, pittore, scultore et architetto*, 32.

"A male child was born to me": Aurelio Gotti, *Vita di Michelangelo Buonarroti, narrata con l'aiuto di nuovi documenti*, vol. 1 (Florence: Gazzetta d'Italia, 1875), 3, https://archive.org/details/vitadimichelange01gott_0.

"the milk of the foster-mother": Condivi, *Michael Angelo Buonarroti*, 6.

"recognized it and was pleased to see it": Vasari, *Lives*, section 1.

"gave him no help whatever": Condivi, *The Life of Michelangelo*, 10.

"Surely you should have known": Vasari, *Lives*, section 2.

"Not only Michael Angelo": Condivi, *Michael Angelo*, 12.

"You will always be poor": Condivi, *Michael Angelo*, 13.

"It was Buonarroti's habit": Benvenuto Cellini, *The Autobiography of Benvenuto Cellini*, trans. John Addington (New York: P. F. Collier & Son, 1910), 24.

"turned his stomach": Condivi, *Michael Angelo*, 81.

Chapter 2

"From what you tell me": Barocchi and Ristori, eds., *Il carteggio di Michelangelo*, I, 7–8, 14 February 1500.

"It will be the most beautiful": Buonarroti, *Le lettere di Michelangelo Buonarroti*, 614.

"keeping always in his mind": Condivi, *Michael Angelo Buonarroti*, 87.

"Between painting and sculpture": Leonardo da Vinci, *Trattato della Pittura*, edited by Angelo Borzelli (Carabba editore, 1947; e-book, 2006), no. 32, www.liberliber.it/mediateca/libri/l/leonardo/trattato_della_pittura/html/index.htm.

"made possible the impossible": Barocchi and Ristori, eds., *Carteggio*, I, 7–8, 14 February 1500.

"I am very glad you are receiving honor": Barocchi and Ristori, eds., *Carteggio*, I, 7–8, 14 February 1500.

"Take special care of your head": Barocchi and Ristori, eds., *Carteggio*, I, 9–10, 19 December 1500.

"to make, carry out and perfectly finish": Buonarroti, *Le lettere*, 620.

Chapter 3

"Nothing the greatest can conceive": Henry Wadsworth Longfellow, "The Artist," in *Complete Poetical Works: Seven Sonnets and a Canzone* (Boston: Houghton, Mifflin, 1893; Bartleby), www.bartleby.com/356 /556.html.

"It's enough to make me believe": Barocchi and Ristori, eds., *Carteggio*, I, 13–14, 2 May 1506.

"better and with more love": Barocchi and Ristori, eds., *Carteggio*, I, 13–14, 2 May 1506.

"terrified": Gaye, *Carteggio inedito d'artisti dei secoli XIV, XV, XVI*, 83, quoted in Spike, *Young Michelangelo: The Path to the Sistine, a Biography*, 207.

"We can assure you": Gaye, *Carteggio inedito*, 91–92, quoted in Spike, *Young Michelangelo*, 215.

"with a rope around my neck": Barocchi and Ristori, eds., *Carteggio*, III, 7–9, December 1523.

"You ought to have come to us": Condivi, *Michael Angelo Buonarroti*, 39.

"You are the ignorant one": Condivi, *Michael Angelo*, 40

"Go to work and keep casting it": Barocchi and Ristori, eds., *Carteggio*, III, 7–9, December 1523.

"I live here in the greatest discomfort": Barocchi and Ristori, eds., *Carteggio*, I, 55–56, 10 November 1507.

"as depressing as can be": Barocchi and Ristori, eds., *Carteggio*, I, 51, 10 August 1507.

"Since I have been here": Barocchi and Ristori, eds., *Carteggio*, I, 51, 10 August 1507.

"Here we are engulfed by armors": Barocchi and Ristori, eds., *Carteggio*, I, 41, 2 May 1507.

Chapter 4

"I am not a painter": Mazur, "Michelangelo: To Giovanni da Pistoia When the Author Was Painting the Vault of the Sistine Chapel," 117.

"a poor thing": Barocchi and Ristori, eds., *Carteggio*, III, 7–9, December 1523.

"I've already grown a goiter": Mazur, "Michelangelo," 116.

"Michelangelo, sculptor": Barocchi and Ristori, eds., *Carteggio*.

"For twelve years now": Michelangelo Buonarroti, *The Letters of Michelangelo*, ed. E. H. Ramsden, vol. I (Stanford: Stanford University Press, 1963), 52.

"since men are worth more than money": Charles Heath Wilson, *Life and Works of Michelangelo Buonarroti* (London: John Murray, 1876), 169.

"in fact relies": Kate Soden, and Sarah Longair, "Teachers' Guide for the BP Special Exhibition Michelangelo Drawings: Closer to the Master 23 March–25 June 2006," British Museum, 8, www .britishmuseum.org/PDF/british_museum_michel angelo_drawings.pdf.

"It brought him so much fame": Condivi, *Michael Angelo Buonarroti*, 42.

"Be at peace": Barocchi and Ristori, eds., *Carteggio*, I, 136, 18 September 1512.

"About the Medici": Barocchi and Ristori, eds., *Carteggio*, I, 139, October 1512.

"If [these measures] don't help": Barocchi and Ristori, eds., *Carteggio*, I, 140–41, October 1512.

Chapter 5

"One must have patience": Michelangelo Buonarroti, *Michelangelo: A Record of His Life as Told in His Own Letters and Papers*, ed. and trans. Robert W. Carsden (London: Constable, 1913), 130–31, https://archive .org/details/michelangeloreco1913mich.

"I shall have to make a great effort": Buonarroti, *Michelangelo*, 91.

"Someone got hurt": Barocchi and Ristori, eds., *Carteggio*, II, 82–83, 13 September 1518.

"broke into a hundred pieces": Barocchi and Ristori, eds., *Carteggio*, II, 185–86, 20 April 1519.

"With regards to art": Barocchi and Ristori, eds., *Carteggio*, III, 1, 25 November 1523.

"Andrea, be patient": On an original drawing in the Ashmolean Museum, Oxford.

"Draw, Antonio": On an original drawing in the British Museum, London.

"the Stick, the Basket": Wallace, *Michelangelo, The Artist, the Man, and His Times*, 140–41.

"made Michelangelo nearly die of laughter": Vasari, *Life of Michelangelo Buonarroti*, 133.

"You are a fool": Vasari, *Life*, 133.

"like a snake's": Condivi, *The Life of Michelangelo*, 106.

"It seems to me": Barocchi and Ristori, eds., *Carteggio*, II, 85, 20 September 1518.

"a knife piercing the heart": Barocchi, Bramanti, and Ristori, eds., *Il carteggio indiretto di Michelangelo*, I, 331, 28 August 1530.

"urged on more by fear," Condivi, *Michael Angelo Buonarroti*, 58.

"Painted like life": Michelangelo Buonarroti, *Selected Poems by Michelangelo Buonarroti, with Translations from Various Sources*, ed. Ednah D. Cheney (Boston: Lee and Shephard, 1885), 141, https://archive.org /details/selectedpoemsfro00michrich.

Chapter 6

"The power to change fate": Buonarroti, *The Poetry of Michelangelo*, 463.

"greatly lamenting": Barocchi and Ristori, eds., *Carteggio*, IV, 13, 12 July 1533.

"For thirty years I have had this wish": Condivi, *The Life of Michelangelo*, 75.

"I am so busy": Barocchi and Ristori, eds., *Carteggio*, IV, 117, 25 August 1541.

"who always see themselves in others": Buonarroti, *Poetry*, 150.

"figures shall not be painted": *The Canons and Decrees of the Council of Trent*, translated by Rev. J. Waterworth (London: C. Dolman, 1848), https://play.google.com/books/reader?id=4K1cAAAAcAAJ&printsec=frontcover&output=reader&hl=en&pg=GBS.PP9.

"the soul and the heart of my fragile life": Buonarroti, *Poetry*, 153.

"They devote no thought": Dante Alighieri, *The Divine Comedy: Paradise*, trans. Allen Mandelbaum (Berkeley: University of California Press, 1980, 1982), canto 29, lines 91–92; "Le opere," Dante Online, English version, www.danteonline.it/italiano/opere.asp?idope=1&idlang=OR.

"Dear to me is sleep": Buonarroti, *Le rime di Michelangelo Buonarroti, pittore, scultore et architetto*, 3.

"without any seriousness and any decorum": Giovanni Andrea Gilio, quoted in Giuseppe Frangi, "The Cappella Paolina by Michelangelo," *30 Days: In the Church and in the World*, August 2009, www.30giorni.it/articoli_id_21545_l3.htm.

Chapter 7

"I serve for the love of God": Richard Duppa, *The Life of Michael Angelo Buonarroti* (London: W. Bulmer, 1816), 191.

"You know": Paul Barolsky, *The Faun in the Garden: Michelangelo and the Poetic Origins of Italian Renaissance Art* (University Park: Pennsylvania State University Press, 1994), 151.

"tragedy": Condivi, *The Life of Michelangelo*, 59, 77.

"Although it is botched and patched up": Condivi, *Michael Angelo Buonarroti*, 68.

"Pope Paul forced me": Barocchi and Ristori, eds., *Carteggio*, V, 105–6, 22 May 1557.

"full, free, and complete permission and authority": Condivi, *The Life of Michelangelo*, 142.

"I have always been": Barocchi and Ristori, eds., *Carteggio*, V, 110–11, 1 July 1557.

"One should have compasses": Vasari, *Life of Michelangelo Buonarroti*, 419.

Chapter 8

"The voyage of my life": Buonarroti, *The Poetry of Michelangelo*, 476.

"I am so old": Condivi, *Michael Angelo Buonarroti*, 235.

"I am able to affirm": John Addington Symonds, *The Life of Michelangelo Buonarroti*, vol. 1 (London, 1893), 101–2.

"In such slavery": Deborah Parker, *Michelangelo and the Art of Letter Writing* (New York: Cambridge University Press 2010), 97.

"[She] loved me": Barocchi and Ristori, eds., *Carteggio*, IV, 344, 1 August 1550.

"high and godly lady": Buonarroti, *Poetry*, 162.

"I can barely write": Barocchi and Ristori, eds., *Carteggio*, V, 55–56, 23 February 1556.

"I am shut up here": Buonarroti, *Poetry*, 452.

"My face has a shape": Buonarroti, *Poetry*, 453.

"tambourines and wrappings": Buonarroti, *Poetry*, 453.

"I think there must be": Barocchi and Ristori, eds., *Carteggio*, IV, 310–11, 1 February 1549.

"health and especially goodness": Barocchi and Ristori, eds., *Carteggio*, IV, 357, 20 December 1550.

"We have to thank [God]": Barocchi and Ristori, eds., *Carteggio*, V, 12, 29 February 1554.

"This is our lot": Barocchi and Ristori, eds., *Carteggio*, V, 12, 29 February 1554.

"What do you want me to do?": Barocchi, Bramanti, and Ristori, eds., *Il carteggio indiretto di Michelangelo*, II, 169–70, 14 February 1564.

"We expect that your Michelangelo": Barocchi, Bramanti, and Ristori, eds., *Carteggio indiretto*, II, 174, 17 February 1564.

"discomforts, fatigue": Barocchi and Ristori, eds., *Carteggio*, I, 9–10, 19 December 1500.

"I believe more in prayers": Barocchi and Ristori, eds., *Carteggio*, IV, 324, 25 April 1549.

"more than a mortal": Ludovico Ariosto, *Orlando Furioso* (Project Gutenberg), canto 33, 2:4, www.gutenberg.org/files/3747/3747-h/3747-h.htm.

SELECTED BIBLIOGRAPHY

Barocchi, Paola, Kathleen Loach Bramanti, and Renzo Ristori, eds. *Il carteggio indiretto di Michelangelo*. Florence: S.P.E.S., 1988–1995; Fondazione Memofonte. www.memofonte .it/autori/carteggio-indiretto-michelangelo -buonarroti-1475-1564.html.

Barocchi, Paola, and Renzo Ristori, eds. *Il carteggio di Michelangelo*. Posthumous edition of G. Poggi. Florence: S.P.E.S., 1965–1983; Fondazione Memofonte. www.memofonte.it /autori/carteggio-michelangelo-buonarroti -1475-1564-10.html.

Buonarroti, Michelangelo. *Le Lettere di Michelangelo Buonarroti*. Edited by Gaetano Milanesi. https://archive.org/details/laletteredimich00 buongoog.

Buonarroti, Michelangelo. *Le rime di Michelangelo Buonarroti, pittore, scultore et architetto*. Edited by Cesare Guasti. Florence: Le Monnier, 1863.

Buonarroti, Michelangelo. *The Poetry of Michelangelo: An Annotated Translation*. Edited by James M. Saslow. New Haven: Yale University Press, 1991.

Condivi, Ascanio. *The Life of Michelangelo*. Edited by Hellmut Wohl. Translated by Alice Sedgwick. University Park: Pennsylvania State University Press, 1999.

Condivi, Ascanio. *Michael Angelo Buonarroti*. Edited by Charles Holroyd. London: Duckworth, 1903; Project Gutenberg, 2006. http: //gutenberg.org/files/19332/19332-h/19332-h .html.

Coonin, Victor A. *From Marble to Flesh: The Biography of Michelangelo's David*. Prato: B'Gruppo, 2014.

Gaye, Johann Wilhelm. *Carteggio inedito d'artisti dei secoli XIV, XV, XVI*. Volume 2. Florence: 1839–1840.

Forcellino, Antonio. *Michelangelo: A Tormented Life*. Translated by Allan Cameron. Maiden, MA: Polity, 2009.

Mazur, Gail. "Michelangelo: To Giovanni da Pistoia When the Author Was Painting the Vault of the Sistine Chapel." In *Zeppo's First Wife: New and Selected Poems*. Chicago: University of Chicago Press, 2005.

Spike, John T., *Young Michelangelo: The Path to the Sistine, a Biography*. New York: Vendome, 2010.

Unger, Miles J., *Michelangelo: A Life in Six Masterpieces*. New York: Simon & Schuster, 2014.

Vasari, Giorgio. *Life of Michelangelo Buonarroti*. Translated by George Bull. London: Folio Society, 1971.

Vasari, Giorgio. *Lives of the Most Eminent Painters, Sculptors and Architects*. Translated by Gaston Du C. De Vere. Volume 9. Part III, "Michelangelo." London: MacMillan, 1912. http://members.efn.org/~acd/vite/VasariMAngelo.html.

Vasari, Giorgio. *Vite de' più eccellenti pittori scultori e architettori*. Edited by Paola Barocchi and R. Bettarini. 1966–1967. First published 1568. www.memofonte.it/home/files/pdf/vasari_vite_giuntina.pdf.

Wallace, William E. *Michelangelo: The Artist, the Man, and His Times*. New York: Cambridge University Press, 2010.

Wallace, William E., *The Genius of Michelangelo*, DVD. The Great Courses. Teaching Company, 2007.

INDEX

Page numbers in *italics* indicate pictures.

ABOUT THE AUTHOR

Simonetta Carr was born in Italy and studied secondary education and art in Milan. She has translated several books from English into Italian and written for newspapers and magazines around the world. She is the award-winning author of the Christian Biographies for Young Readers series, which includes *John Calvin*, *Augustine of Hippo*, and others.

Also available from Chicago Review Press

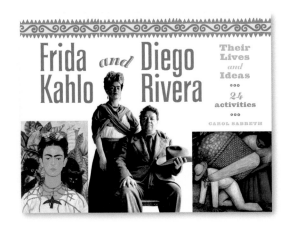

Frida Kahlo and Diego Rivera
Their Lives and Ideas, 24 Activities

Carol Sabbeth

$17.95 (CAN $25.95)
9781556525698
Also available in e-book formats

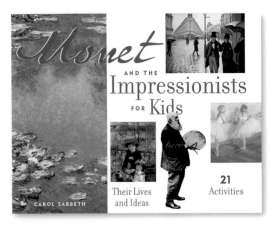

Monet and the Impressionists for Kids
Their Lives and Ideas, 21 Activities

Carol Sabbeth

$17.95 (CAN $26.95)
9781556523977
Also available in e-book formats

"A compelling introduction to this 19th-century movement."

—*Publishers Weekly*

Leonardo da Vinci for Kids
His Life and Ideas, 21 Activities

Janis Herbert

$17.95 (CAN $19.95)
9781556522987
Also available in e-book formats

"The high-quality reproductions of the artist's sketches and paintings coupled with an interesting text give readers a full picture of this truly amazing man."

—*School Library Journal*

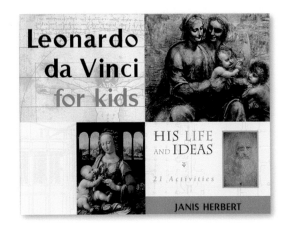

Salvador Dalí and the Surrealists
Their Lives and Ideas, 21 Activities

Michael Elsohn Ross

$17.95 (CAN $26.95)
9781556524790
Also available in e-book formats

"Visually stunning…eminently readable, the crisply written text is detailed and thorough…. A valuable addition to any collection."

—*School Library Journal*

CHICAGO REVIEW PRESS

Distributed by IPG
www.ipgbook.com

www.chicagoreviewpress.com

Available at your favorite bookstore, by calling (800) 888-4741, or at www.chicagoreviewpress.com

Van Gogh and the Post-Impressionists for Kids
Their Lives and Ideas, 21 Activities

Carol Sabbeth

$17.95 (CAN $19.95)
9781569762752
Also available in e-book formats

"This book is an excellent resource for students and teachers. The extensive biographical information not only provides solid material for school reports, but also makes for a truly fascinating read."

—*School Library Journal*